Learning Spaces

SRHE and Open University Press Imprint

Current titles include:

Learning Spaces

Creating Opportunities for Knowledge
Creation in Academic Life

Maggi Savin-Baden

 Society for Research into Higher Education
& Open University Press

Open University Press
McGraw-Hill Education
McGraw-Hill House
Shoppenhangers Road
Maidenhead
Berkshire
England
SL6 2QL

email: enquiries@openup.co.uk
world wide web: www.openup.co.uk

and Two Penn Plaza, New York, NY 10121-2289, USA

First published 2008

A catalogue record of this book is available from the British Library

ISBN-10 0 335 22230 7 (pb)   0 335 22231 5 (hb)
ISBN-13: 978 0 335 22230 8 (pb)   978 0 335 22231 5 (hb)

Library of Congress Cataloging-in-Publication Data
CIP data has been applied for

Typeset by RefineCatch Limited, Bungay, Suffolk
Printed in the UK by Bell and Bain Ltd Glasgow

The **McGraw·Hill** Companies

For Zak

Contents

Acknowledgements

Thanks are due to a number of people: Tamsin Haggis, Becca Khanna, Jon Nixon and Christine Sinclair for their helpful, enthusiastic and critical comments on the manuscript. To Ron Barnett for the encouragement to develop this book further than my first thoughts and Shona Mullen, Managing Director, McGraw-Hill Education for her support and guidance during this project.

Thanks also to Lana and Hennie van Niekerk for providing me with a beautiful writing space at their home in Cape Town.

My immense thanks are also due to John Savin-Baden for his support, critique, proofreading and indexing.

The views expressed here and any errors are mine.

Introduction

This book emerged from my own concern about ways of finding and creating spaces for my own development as an academic. This, for me, was not just about attending courses nor 'doing' continuous professional development; it was about finding spaces to write, think, reflect and engage with my current and often changing position on issues in higher education. Space creation sometimes related to grappling with articles I was reading or speeches I had heard, but more often than that it was about positioning my self in relation to what was being said.

The ability to have or to find space in academic life seems to be increasingly difficult since we seem to be consumed by teaching and bidding, overwhelmed by emails and underwhelmed by long arduous meetings. While I realize that there are many academics who enjoy this hurly-burly lifestyle, and even those who like to be supremely busy because it helps to avoid the anguish and endurance of research and writing, it has become apparent that this busyness seems to be stifling creativity and academic thought. While it is important to recognize that ideas and thoughts are often generated and prompted through discussions and meetings, it is also essential that space for reflecting, thinking and writing are seen as important for the development of academe and the positioning of the academic self within it. Currently there seems to a lack of realization that we are losing ground because we are losing space.

This book explores the concept of learning spaces, the idea that there are diverse forms of spaces within the life and life world of the academic where opportunities to reflect and critique their own unique learning position occur. The kinds of spaces I am referring to, while also physical, are largely seen as mental and metaphorical. In such spaces, staff often recognize that their perceptions of learning, teaching, knowledge and learner identity are being challenged and realize that they have to make a decision about their own responses to such challenges. Yet these often hidden spaces are invariably not valued by university leadership and industrious colleagues nor recognized as being important in our media-populated culture. This volume sets out to challenge notions and expectations that ideas and thoughts really can be generated in cramped, overpopulated offices, awash with email and a constant stream of people, and argues instead for a need to recognize, promote and even (re-)create new and different opportunities for learning spaces to emerge in academic life. Through this book I therefore argue that:

1. Learning spaces are increasingly absent in academic life.
2. The creation and re-creation of learning spaces is vital for the survival of the academic community.
3. The absence of learning spaces is resulting in increasing dissolution and fragmentation of academic identities.
4. Learning spaces need to be valued and possibly redefined in order to regain and maintain the intellectual health of academe.

This volume is divided into three parts. Part 1, Re-viewing the Landscape, begins in Chapter 1 by presenting the notion of learning spaces and examining ideas and literature related to this concept. It outlines different forms of learning spaces, and examines both the relationship between these spaces and their impact on each other. Chapter 2 suggests ways in which learning spaces may be created, not just in terms of creating time and space for oneself, but as a way of living in the academic community.

Part 2, entitled Engaging Possibilities, outlines different forms of learning spaces in detail. It begins in Chapter 3 by discussing the importance of writing spaces. While there is a large body of academics who can and do already write copious amounts, there has been little in-depth discussion about how academics become successful publishers or how they develop spaces in which to write. This chapter discusses ways of not only creating writing spaces, but also of supporting staff to learn to speak for themselves and to create a 'writing voice'. The notion of learning through dialogue is not new but the notion of dialogic spaces is a concept that is presented and explored in Chapter 4. This chapter examines the importance of dialogue as a learning space, arguing that discussion is an important site for learning and that the development of intellectual ideas is one that is increasingly overlooked by academics. Chapter 5 then explores the notion of reflective spaces, spaces that are often given much currency in the professional education of students, but perhaps not used a great deal by staff. This chapter examines the extent to which reflection can be both enabling and disabling in the process of developing ideas, and scrutinizes the literature on reflection which to date remains largely anecdotal and under-researched. Chapter 6 considers digital spaces and the way in which electronic communication has created different spaces for learning, discussion and knowledge creation than in former years. This chapter also considers the way in which electronic learning environments can be constricted spaces as a result of the over-management of the learning space. Chapter 7 presents the idea of troublesome spaces as places where 'stuckness' occurs. For both academics and students, becoming stuck in learning is often seen as deeply problematic rather than as useful and transformative learning space. This chapter explores notions of troublesomeness, liminality and disjunction, suggesting that we need to explore the fractures in our pedagogies.

Finally Part 3, Transforming Locations, offers some possibilities for the future by arguing for the creation of transformative spaces. It begins in Chapter 8 by considering boundary spaces, those spaces within civic society, between cultures and politics, between people and institutions and between diverse forms of knowledges. It is only by understanding these spaces that universities and academics can engage or re-engage with their various publics. Chapter 9 then examines the notion of spatial identities. The focus here is not only on how academics portray themselves in digital spaces, but also the changes that occur to identity in new learning spaces. This section draws on research into changes in an academic identity through engaging in new and re-created learning spaces, and presents participants' views relating to issues of transformation. The final chapter of this volume argues that if the university is to maintain some leverage in the world of intellectual thought, it needs to regain learning spaces as places in which in-depth deliberation and intellectual positioning can occur.

This book, then, is an attempt to gather together some thoughts about the relationship between a number of ideas and concepts, and I feel the learning space in which I am currently located is somewhat liminal. However, it is a text that seeks to engage with the disjunction prompted by the notion of learning spaces, just as perhaps one of Faulks's characters, Sonia, was at the end of his novel:

> There were questions to which her husband and brother had bent their minds – had sent themselves as good as mad trying to answer; but it seemed to Sonia at that moment, drenched and tired as she was, that, perhaps for quite simple reasons connected to the limits of their ability to reason, human beings could live out their whole life long without ever knowing what sort of creatures they really were. Perhaps it did not matter; perhaps what was important was to find serenity in not knowing.
> (Faulks, 2005: 609)

Part 1

Re-viewing the Landscape

1
Forms of Learning Spaces

Introduction

This chapter presents the notion of learning spaces and explores ideas and literature related to this concept. It outlines different forms of learning spaces, and examines the relationship between different kinds of learning spaces and the impact one may have on another. The first section of the chapter examines a range of understandings of space and draws on the work of a number of theorists. It focuses on Lefebvre's notions of space (Lefebvre, 1991) and explores the concepts of smooth and striated space as outlined by Deleuze and Guattari (1988). The second section presents the notion of learning spaces and explores how they might be located, understood and engaged with in the context of the academy.

Delineating learning spaces

The concept of learning spaces expresses the idea that there are diverse forms of spaces within the life and life world of the academic where opportunities to reflect and analyse their own learning position occur. The notion of life world is based on both Husserl (1937/1970) and Habermas (1987) and represents the idea that as human beings we have a culturally transmitted stock of taken-for-granted perspectives and interpretations that are organized in a communicative way. Such learning spaces are places of engagement where often disconnected thoughts and ideas, that have been inchoate, begin to cohere as a result of the creation of some kind of suspension from daily life. In such spaces, staff often recognize that their perceptions of learning, teaching, knowledge and identity are being challenged and realize that they have to make a decision about their response to such challenges. Yet such often hidden spaces are invariably not valued by university leadership and industrious colleagues, nor recognized as being important in our media-populated culture.

The consideration of learning spaces presented here emerged from a real-ization that my most generative work occurred at times in my academic life when I was dislocated from the 'noise' of the academic community in which I worked. Phipps (2005) has discussed the notion of 'sounds' in academia and argues that the changes in sounds are having a somewhat unhelpful impact on the quality of academic life experiences. Phipp's work, although located in a deconstruction of sounds, in many ways refers to the impact of noise on learning spaces. For example, understandings and constructions of the concept of learning spaces argued for in this book are seen not only as the creation of mental and physical dislocation from academic noise, but also as the location or creation of spaces in which one can hear things differently. Learning spaces may be, and often are, different for each person, in diverse ways at contrasting points in their lives, but it seems there are some common elements that occur in the interstices and the overlaps of people's experiences. Common types of learning spaces may occur through:

- Physical and/or psychological removal from the normal learning environ-ment. For example, attending conferences, writing retreats or working overseas. New environments often prompt new ways of seeing issues, pro-viding opportunities for reflection and presenting challenges to current ways of thinking
- The creation of specific time for writing or reflection
- Using social learning spaces for dialogue and debate
- Accessing digital spaces for discussion and reflection with and through others.

The notion of learning spaces, then, stretches beyond the idea of just finding or making time to think and write. The kinds of spaces I am referring to include the physical spaces in which we place ourselves, but what is important, vital even, about learning spaces is that they have a different kind of temporality and different ways of thinking. Authors such as Baudrillard (1994) have discussed the space/time implosion, and perhaps more help-fully, Castells (1996). Castells argued that flows of capital, information, tech-nology, organizational interaction, images, sounds and symbols go from one disjointed position to another and gradually replace a space of locales 'whose form, function and meaning are self-contained within the boundaries of physical contiguity' (Castells, 1996: 423). Space is inseparable from time; it is 'crystallized time' (Castells, 1996: 411). What I am referring to is not merely about managing time, finding time or rearranging one's day, although these are important factors in working towards what Eriksen refers to as 'slow time' (Eriksen, 2001: 50). Instead I am arguing for locating oneself in spaces where ideas and creativity can grow and flourish, spaces where being with our thoughts offers opportunities to rearrange them in spaces where the values of being are more central than the values of doing.

Learning spaces are often places of transition, and sometimes transform-ation, where the individual experiences some kind of shift or reorientation in their life world. Engagement in learning spaces does not necessarily result in the displacement of identity (in the sense of a shift causing such a sense of disjunction that it results in costs personally and pedagogically, and hence has a life cost) but rather a shift in identity or role perception so that issues and concerns are seen and heard in new and different ways. Learning spaces might also be seen as liminal in nature in that they can be seen as betwixt and between states that generally occur because of a particular need of an individual to gain or create a learning space.

Notions of space

There has been an increasing interest in the notion of space in higher education and more recently on physical space. For example, a study funded by the Higher Education Academy in the UK has undertaken a literature review to 'inform the design of learning spaces for the future, to facilitate changing pedagogical practices to support a mass higher education system, and greater student diversity' (Temple et al., 2007). The review focuses on research into the built environment; the organizational nature of higher education in terms of how universities are governed and managed, including changing relations with their students, research relating to how students learn and factors influencing the learning process. However, there has been relatively little consideration of the ways in which space is seen both as a site of learning and more particularly as a site of power. Universities and university leadership in particular seem to take little notice of the understandings, formulations and functions of space. For instance, the social architecture of universities tends to represent different ideologies – the lecture theatres of tradition and knowledge, the carpets and beanbags of innovation. Yet the control of space and the way in which it is valued and represented is evident through timetables, meetings, teaching and office spaces and organizational practices. This very ordering belies the way that university learning spaces shape not only student learning and staff practices, but also the very nature of higher education itself, as Lefebvre has argued: '*(Social) space is a (social) product* . . . space thus produced also serves as a tool of thought and of action; that in addition to being a means of production it is also a means of control, and hence domination, of power; yet that as such escapes in part from those who would make use of it' (Lefebvre, 1991: 26, original emphasis). However, there are other kinds of spaces that are part of, but also overlay the notion of learning spaces. For example, Lefebvre (1991) has suggested social space might be seen as comprising of a conceptual triad of spatial practice, representations of space and representational spaces.

Spatial practice represents the way in which space is produced and reproduced in particular locations and social formations. Yet it is a space that is located between daily routine and the practices and infrastructure of daily life that affect it, impact on it and ultimately organize it. This formulation of space has created spatial zones and imaginary geographies; boundaries around conceptions of time and space have moved and so we have created different kinds of 'spaces'. For example, learning, knowledge, relationships, communication, home and work places are no longer seen by staff and students as static, bounded and uniform but instead as ongoing, variable and emergent.

Representations of space are related to the relationships between sites of production and the way in which signs and codes are used within those representations. These spaces are conceived spaces and are the spaces of the planners and architects. These 'real' spaces are defined by the physical world, such as the design of the buildings and the space that exists between and within structures shaped by the organization's function and activity – past and present. With the rise of telework there is now a shift towards a notion of *flexible spaces* in homes, therefore the notion of representations of space no longer engenders an integrated idea of the use of space but, rather, is a space of change.

Representational spaces embody symbolisms, some of which may be coded, but importantly the representation is linked to what is hidden, what is clandestine. The notion of representational spaces is symbolized by activities that necessarily occur within them, while at the same time they embody complexity and symbolism. Representational spaces are not therefore integrated concepts, but symbolic and covert. Put more simply, representational spaces can be seen in formulations of lived spaces, which may, for example, change according to the weather when workers move indoors from the outside office (shed). Alternatively it may change with time when the children go to bed and the laptop is put on the kitchen worktop so that one partner can work while the other cooks. In the main, domestic life tends to shape representational space in the home, yet with the blurring of boundaries between home and work the meaning of 'lived space' and the symbolism attached to particularly areas of representational space have shifted. Yet this understanding of representational space remains problematic when the change in use of a space is not recognized by all who utilize that space. For example, many complaints are made about learning groups in campus bars and about the noise in the library – the latter is no longer a symbolic, nor an actual, silent workspace.

Lefebvre's constitution of spaces, along with territorial, disciplinary and institutional spaces impact on learning spaces by preventing the development of creative spaces, yet an understanding of the diversity and complexity of learning spaces can also inform the ways that they are (re-)created and managed. For example, spaces between people and places are important learning spaces.

Territorial spaces: the spaces between the tribes of academia, whether disciplinary tribes or departmental tribes, are places in which understandings about issues of power, status and emphasis are important. For example, academics who wish to appoint new staff quickly become impatient with the practices of the personnel department where issues of law and equity are primary human resource concerns. Further, the concerns of the managers to promote the profile of the university and manage the purse effectively are seen as important sites, but for many staff the gaining of research grants and the effectiveness of their teaching are more important territories.

Space between learner and teacher: the concerns and agendas of staff and students are inevitably different spaces with diverse emphases, but such spaces are often complex and difficult to manage. Often these spaces are not just different in territory but also in language and social practices. The notion of *translation* is perhaps useful here in understanding the complexity of these forms of space. Translation is normally seen as finding parallels between two languages or as a means of mediation between languages. Yet in the process of translation, words, discourse and practices change and their meanings are often mislaid and misunderstood. The difficulty with attempting to translate academics' ideas into something simplified and accessible to students often makes matters worse, but perhaps the ways of managing these spaces between learners and teachers should not be managed through translation, but as Burbules has suggested, through acknowledging that there are no clear lines, except for those of uncertainty and difficulty:

> We must move from the idea of a translation to the idea of an aporetic encounter – finding our way through a labyrinth with no clear lines to follow. Uncertainty, difficulty, and discomfort in such an encounter are intrinsic. And because the failure of translation in practical contexts of communication is related to the inability to act or coordinate action, such difficulties are *moral* difficulties as well. The challenge of moral responsiveness in the face of radical difference is as much a part of the feeling of aporia as are epistemic or linguistic limits. Here even the possibility of communication, let alone translation, is put at risk. (Burbules, 1997: 5, original emphasis)

Spaces between learners: with the changes in higher education over the past 30 years, particularly with the global widening of access, it is acknowledged that the student body comprises greater diversity than in former years. Although much has been done to support this in terms of mathematics and literacy support units and academic writing centres, difficulties still arise. Acknowledging the importance of learning spaces introduces questions to do with our understandings of learner conception, stances and experiences, and prompts considerations about expectations and assumptions about students. For example, there is a tendency in higher education to make assumptions that students have similar wants, needs, aspirations and approaches to learning. Haggis has argued:

> If it is accepted that students are likely to be different both from each other and from academics themselves, then there are arguably problems with assumptions such as the following:
>
> - that it is acceptable practice to give out a reading list or set of essay questions expecting that students will know how to think, read and write in response to these
> - that university teaching is, and should be, about exploring and

conveying key features of disciplinary content, rather than examining and modelling processes of thought and ways of interacting with/ producing texts

- that essay feedback which refers to 'structure', 'evidence' and 'argument' is transparent and self-explanatory. (Haggis, 2004: 349–50)

Such differences must be acknowledged as we design more innovative learning spaces that meet the needs and aspirations of learners and teachers. Further, in the process of such engagement it is vital that we also acknowledge the importance of how 'texts' are conceived of, used and managed in academic life.

Textual spaces are spaces in which 'texts' must be engaged with in academic life. Texts here include not only written or digital texts but also the text of lectures, tutorials and seminars. While this area of textuality and understanding of text has been much discussed in literacy and academic writing fields, the notion of the 'imported text' (Boughey, 2006) is one that is discussed little between academics. Understanding what counts as a text and the space in which such texts are located are important sites of dialogic understanding. For example, rules of academic engagement, particularly related to disciplinary rules, pedagogical signatures and discipline-based pedagogy are located both within and beyond the text. Yet these spaces are problematic because of the ways in which staff interpret for each other, and for students. As staff create and re-create textual spaces for students, they often ignore students' choices, the choice to disengage with the rules, such as working for a pass rather than a 'good' degree or leaving the course because it prevents them from engaging with particular social practices they believe in. There is often a sense that academics within disciplines forget that texts are not asocial, apolitical and that in drawing on text we draw on located contexts. It is through dialogue that engagement with texts and textual spaces are constructed, which is discussed in Chapter 3 and Chapter 4.

However, learning spaces can be 'created' spaces', spaces that just occur or 'unexpected' learning spaces such as:

- Bounded learning spaces: days away in which to think and reflect, alone or in a group
- Formal learning spaces: courses and conferences
- Social learning spaces: where dialogue and debate can occur in informal and less bounded settings
- Silent learning spaces: away from 'sounds' that get in the way of creativity, innovation and space to think
- Writing spaces: places not only to write but to reconsider one's stances and ideas
- Dialogic spaces: in which critical conversations can occur but also where the relationship between the oral and the written can be explored
- Reflective learning spaces: which reach beyond contemplation and reconsidering past thoughts, they are spaces of meaning-making, and consciousness-raising

- Digital learning spaces: where explorations occur about new types of visuality, literacy, pedagogy, representations of knowledge, communication and embodiment.

Learning spaces as smooth and striated cultural spaces

Learning spaces could then be delineated in particular ways, seen as bounded by time, place, institutional and disciplinary culture. However, work by Deleuze and Guattari is helpful in examining learning spaces from a different perspective to those already considered in this chapter. They argue for smooth and striated cultural spaces. For them the notion of smooth space is one of becoming, it is a nomadic space where the movement is more important than the arrival. Whereas in a striated space, the focal point is one of arrival, arrival at the point towards which one is oriented: 'In striated space, lines or trajectories tend to be subordinated to points: one goes from one point to another. In the smooth, it is the opposite: the points are subordinated to the trajectory' (Deleuze and Guattari, 1988: 478). Striated learning spaces and smooth learning spaces are depicted below in somewhat stark utopian terms in order to illustrate their difference. However, as will be seen later in the chapter, there is doubtless more overlap than is immediately suggested here.

Striated learning spaces

These spaces are characterized by a strong sense of organization and boundedness. Learning in such spaces is epitomized though course attendance, defined learning places such as lecture theatres and classrooms, and with the use of (often set) books. These spaces may not be necessarily located in an institution – the learning spaces may be in the work place. However, what is common to these kinds of spaces is the strong sense of authorship, a sense of clear definition, of outcomes, of a point that one is expected to reach. Such spaces are therefore authored in design (whether inked or virtual) and in the way they are enacted in classroom practices, with a sense of subordination to a body of knowledge and the power of the expert. In such spaces students will be expected, for example, to take notes in lectures and learn and subsume disciplinary practices, rather than challenge them.

Smooth learning spaces

Smooth learning spaces are open, flexible and contested, spaces in which both learning and learners are always on the move. Students here would be encouraged to contest knowledge and ideas proffered by lecturers and in doing so create their own stance toward knowledge(s). Yet the movement is not towards a given trajectory, instead, there is a sense of displacement of notions of time and place so that the learning space is not defined, but becomes defined by the creator of the space. The location of learning spaces in a variety of sites and spheres results in the learner and learning being displaced from and within striated contexts, and therefore such displacement might be seen by some academics and managers as dubious and risky. Moreover, such displacement also involves new and shifting ways of placing one's self in smooth learning spaces, which may be troublesome since such learning spaces become a constant challenge to identity and may result in a recurrent sense of disjunction. Students located in smooth spaces may be seen as a threat to the stability of disciplinary practices because their disjunction will prompt them to question what is allowed and disallowed within the discipline. For this reason smooth learning spaces are often seen as suspect, or as privileged spaces for the undisciplined, and to be partisan about such activity can set up challenges to other academics about what counts as legitimate learning space. However, this is not to say that striated spaces cannot contain smooth spaces, yet when they do this presents difficulties about the relationship between the two spaces and the relative value of each.

The interplay of striated and smooth learning spaces

The contrast between smooth and striated learning spaces introduces questions about the role and identity of universities and academics in terms of what counts as a legitimate learning space and who makes such decisions of legitimacy. For many academics, the boundaries between smooth and striated learning spaces will be troublesome because smooth spaces are not always without boundaries but instead are framed differently. For example, in striated learning spaces, it is possible to frame the learning in terms of conference or course attendance, the striated space is clear – although the smoothness within it may not be. Yet undefined scholarly activity where the purpose is to think and write is invariably complex and contested, particularly given that a feature of smooth learning spaces is flexibility, a characteristic increasingly subsumed by busyness and accountability in a performative academic culture. The 'difference' associated with smooth spaces means that they will be problematic locations to inhabit and the opportunity for disjunction to occur is likely. Many staff have described disjunction as being a little like hitting a brick wall, there is an overwhelming sense of 'stuckness' and they have then used various strategies to try to deal with it. It has similarities with troublesome knowledge; Perkins (1999: 10) describes conceptually difficult knowledge as 'troublesome knowledge'. This is knowledge that appears, for example, counter-intuitive, alien (emanating from another culture or discourse) or incoherent (discrete aspects are unproblematic but there is no organizing principle). Disjunction, then, is not only a form of troublesome knowledge but also a 'space' or 'position' reached through the realization that the knowledge is troublesome. Disjunction might therefore be seen as a 'troublesome learning space' that emerges from smooth learning spaces, indeed Deleuze and Guattari, have argued: 'Of course, smooth spaces are not in themselves liberatory. But the struggle is changed or displaced in them, and life reconstitutes its stakes, confronts new obstacles, invents new paces, switches adversaries. Never believe that a smooth space will suffice to save us' (Deleuze and Guattari, 1988: 500).

However, at the same time there is a sense that smooth and striated spaces also pervade one another, and possibly emerge from each other and invade one another. This sense of pervasion and appropriation brings with it a sense that subversion occurs in both spaces. Thus, there is a sense that whatever one does to subvert striated spaces, routines and rituals will still be enacted and re-enacted. For example, authors such as Rosenberg (1994) have argued that hypertext is both art and pedagogy, but despite this both creator and user can only re-enact logocentrism since hypertext is necessarily driven by its rules and system. While there are many such cogent arguments, what is problematic about many of them is the assumption that identities are always necessarily 'positioned' by the way in which such spaces are created. Certainly, Bayne's insightful analysis (Bayne, 2005b) suggests virtual learning environments (VLEs) such as WebCT affirm notions of how teaching and learning *should* be. As Cousin (2005: 121) has pointed out too, these VLEs are fraught with images that are deeply problematic, such as 'a little white male professor' that adorns WebCT as its premier logo. These images of scaffolding, structure and safety suggest stability and control. Further, these systems also encourage staff not only to manage knowledge, but also to manage discussions and possibly even to think and teach in linear ways. Clearly, in such striated spaces one is 'being' positioned. Yet to position one's self in a smooth learning space in a striated learning environment is surely to position oneself as other than one is expected to 'be'. If, however, there are possibilities for the creation of smooth spaces in striated environments, then there needs to be an acknowledgement that we are aware of the ways in which striated spaces and systems have moulded our assumptions, perceptions and pedagogies. Such perspective transformation will mean that it is possible to see and use striated spaces differently and critically, while acknowledging which interruption, disruption and disturbance, which are features of smooth spaces, will continue to render the smooth on the striated intensely problematic.

Learning spaces as the construction of pedagogy?

It is argued in this section that learning spaces offer opportunities to re-examine and possibly reconstruct our disciplinary and institutional pedagogies. Such opportunities might occur by examining conceptions of learning and teaching, by shifting from notions of generalizable learning styles to identity-located learning stances and by embracing the idea of spatial ecology in the context of higher education. Spatial ecology is defined here as the creation of balance between and across spaces in higher education, so that account is taken of not merely knowledge, content, conceptions and acquisition, but also of ontology, of values and beliefs, uncertainty and complexity.

Learning stances

It is suggested here that instead of adopting conceptions of learning or learning styles it is vital that learning is located with/in the identities of the learner. In the early 2000s there has been increasing debate about the value of learning styles, although as an idea they remain popular with many in staff development and in business communities. To move away from the idea of learning styles removes possibilities for generalizing learner approaches and instead presents the notion that learning is complex and specific to the learner and must therefore be located in the context of their lives and their stories. This is discussed in more detail in Chapter 2. The notion of stance is used here to indicate that the learners, at different times and in different spaces, 'locate' themselves as individual learners. To some extent stances in and towards learning are invariably formulated through school experiences and parental expectations. However, this model of learning stances (Savin-Baden, 2000) stands against the notion of learning styles and deep and surface approaches, arguing instead that stances relate not only to cognitive perspectives but also to ontological positioning within learning environments. Conflict between expectation, identity and belief in a learning context can result in staff and students becoming stuck: experiencing disjunction in learning and in teaching, either personally, pedagogically or interactionally.

Stance is used here in the sense of one's attitude, belief or disposition towards a particular context, person or experience. It refers to a particular position one takes up in life towards something, at a particular point in time. Stance is not just a matter of attitude; it encompasses our unconscious beliefs and prejudices, our prior learning experiences, our perceptions of tutors, peers and learning situations, and our past, present and future selves. Each stance contains a number of domains and movement between them is diverse, depending on each individual and set of circumstances. The borders of the domains are somewhat blurred, as in the edges of colours in the spectrum. Movement can take place within domains as well as across them.

The stances are presented in Figure 1.1 and are defined briefly as follows:

- Personal stance: the way in which staff and students see themselves in relation to the learning context and give their own distinctive meaning to their experience of that context

- Pedagogical stance: the ways in which people see themselves as learners in particular educational environments
- Interactional stance: the ways in which learners work and learn in groups and construct meaning in relation to one another.

My research into students' experiences found that transitions in students' personal, pedagogical and interactional stances were often sites of struggle (Savin-Baden, 2000). For example, students who had previously experienced learning as knowledge that was located by and defined through the teacher, experienced a challenge to their pedagogical stance when faced with seeing knowledge as something that was to be contested in the context of problem-based learning. Transitions were sometimes difficult and disturbing; yet in many cases they were places where personal change took place. Yet students did not just have a stance, it was something that they constructed and which related to issues of identity, relationships with others and the learning context. Staff stances also impact not only on student learning, but on other staff and on staff's own identities as teachers. In particular, staff pedagogical stances affect the kinds of teaching and learning opportunities they offer and the types of learning behaviour they affirm and reward. The choices and interventions that tutors make within a learning environment and the particular concerns they bring to a learning environment all emerge from their pedagogical stances. Tutors' stances emerge from their prior learning experiences, and their often taken-for-granted notions of learning

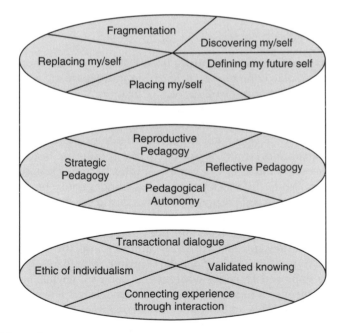

Figure 1.1 Learning stances

and teaching. The four domains within the concept of pedagogical stance are reproductive pedagogy, strategic pedagogy, pedagogical autonomy and reflective pedagogy:

- *Reproductive pedagogy* staff see themselves as the suppliers of all legitimate knowledge and therefore as facilitators they act as gap fillers.
- *Strategic pedagogy* staff employ tactics that prompt in students cue-seeking behaviour.
- *Pedagogical autonomy* staff enable students to meet their own personally defined needs as learners, while also ensuring that they will pass the course.
- *Reflective pedagogy* staff help students to realize that learning is a flexible entity and that there are also other valid ways of seeing things besides their own perspective.

It is important to note that the borders of the domains merge with one another, and therefore shifts between domains represent transitional areas where particular kinds of transitional learning and teaching occur. Further, it is important to note that movement across domains within a stance can occur from one domain to any other and that transitions between domains is not ordered or hierarchical in any way. In the context of learning spaces, staff need to recognize and explore their own pedagogical stances in order to examine the impact they have on the learning context and student stances and experiences.

Spatial ecology

The difficulty associated with locating both learners and teachers as possessing only a particular conception of learning and teaching, is that it seems to imply a deficiency model of higher education. This suggests that they only have the ability to see, understand and locate particular components, and therefore the perspectives and knowledge they have gained are then at best only partial. To accept such models is to accept the view that learning styles and conception largely represent what people *are not* and *have not*, rather than seeing them as operating in complex systems located in a diverse spatial ecology. While the model of learning stances could be seen as being overly simplistic, it not only represents learners and teachers as having more than one style, but also a spatial locale from which they operate. Thus the notion of spatial ecology reflects the idea that staff and students come to understand how they interact with one another and the various learning spaces in which they live, work and learn. Further, to date much of the literature that has explored learning context has been somewhat narrowly construed. For example, Ramsden (1984; 1992) suggested learning context is created through students' experience of the constituents of the programmes on which they are studying, namely, teaching methods, assessment mechanisms and the overall design of the curriculum. Whereas spatial ecology is a concept which captures the sense of there needing to be a balance between and across spaces in higher education, so that account is taken of not merely knowledge, content, conceptions and acquisition but also of ontology, values and beliefs, uncertainty and complexity.

The idea of spatial ecology captures the idea that it is recognized that staff and students operate on diverse trajectories and when they collide learning spaces emerge and often learning occurs. For example, differences in staff and students' stances towards particular concepts such as family or gender prompt staff and students to consider the diverse spaces in which they live, work and learn and the impact of their life world on their learning. It is through discussion and exploration that notions of translation, shifting spaces and spaces of representation along with diverse and difficult territorial positions are recognized. Yet in order to create learning spaces in which it is possible to realize chronic uncertainty, there is also recognition that a tentative balance occurs through which staff and students come to manage learning. As learners and teachers we are not apolitical, acultural or disembodied beings, but we are often disturbed and uncomfortable, and need to have a sense of how our presuppositions impact on and interact with those of others in other spaces.

Learning spaces as an ide*a*logy

Barnett (2003) has argued that ideologies have entered and taken a grip on universities in ways that are both virtuous and pernicious, but that it is not possible to remove such ideologies. He suggests that what is needed is the development of positive ideologies, which he terms 'idealogies' that can prevent the corrosion of positive ideologies and which embrace and promote the ideals the university possesses. 'Amid the ideologies that threaten to overwhelm it, the university can find itself again through virtuous idealogies. Such ide*a*logies call for a leadership that can stand apart from the rhythms of the age and can forge alternative sources of *being* in the university' (Barnett, 2003: 131, original emphasis). Barnett therefore argues for qualities such as reasonableness, and willingness to learn, which will enable the university to operate in, and with a flexible structure in, the context of a fluid world. In order to shift from ideology to ide*a*logy it is important to recognize the increasing number of performative practices, which pervade the lives of students and academics. These focus on Bloom (1956), behaviourism, lesson plans and learning outcomes and are surely mechanisms that regulate and delimit learning spaces. Just as the focus on outcomes pedagogy has created a particular type of curriculum, this pedagogy has also occluded academics' visions about possible alternatives. Curricula designed using behavioural objectives rather than learning intentions close down opportunities for creative and innovative forms of learning, and in turn occlude the vision to create smooth learning spaces. Pernicious performativity pervades judgement, and academics see themselves as being required to replicate the same narrow practices in their own learning spaces. For example, Nespor has argued that the notion of the classroom being 'center' is:

> an image at once familiar and problematic: there are, after all, different kinds of centers, from cherry pits to doughnut holes. On the one hand, many researchers – and policymakers in the U.S. government – adopt what could be called an 'internalist' perspective, in which the classroom is treated as a bounded container of teaching and learning – it's a center in the sense that the important things are endogenously generated there and then transferred or moved outwards. (Nespor, 2006: 1)

However, those individuals who choose to adopt such striated positions invariably engage less with learning spaces and those with which they do engage are more likely to be formal and principally striated in nature. Yet it might also be the case that those who create smooth learning spaces are those who value reflection and so work to shore up and sustain a nomadic academic identity. As Deleuze and Guattari assert, 'one is never "in front of"', any more than one is "in" smooth space – rather, one is "on" it' (1988: 493). Yet similarly, students would not say they are 'in' a course, rather they are 'on' it, they and we are essentially always part of a structure or a curriculum. There are some similarities here with Bayne's critique of virtual learning environments, where she argues 'e-learning systems promise "seamlessness" of integration with other university information systems – the elimination of gaps into the unregulated unknown and the delimiting of space is their very purpose' (Bayne, 2004: 313). Despite this there seem to be instances where unexpected learning spaces emerge. For example, there is evidence that learning spaces can occur in the process of role transition, such as shifting from the role of a lecturer to a facilitator of learning. Earlier work (Savin-Baden, 2003) illustrates how staff experiences of role change resulted in unexpected shifts. For many staff engaged in interactive forms of learning, the transition from lecturer to facilitator demanded revising their assumptions about what it means to be a teacher in higher education. This is a challenge to many since it invariably demands recognition of a loss of power and control when moving towards being a facilitator. The conflict for many staff is in allowing students to manage knowledge for themselves, when staff have in previous roles and relationships with students been the controllers and patrollers of knowledge. For example, the catalyst for transition for many staff becoming involved in problem-based learning has been attending a course designed to equip them to be facilitators of problem-based learning seminars (see, for example, Savin-Baden, 2003). Although such courses are invariably striated learning spaces, many seminar participants found smooth learning spaces also occurred on the striated ones; therefore the notion of transition within learning spaces is an important concern. As Deleuze and Guattari have argued, 'it is possible to live striated on the deserts, steppes, or seas; it is possible to live smooth even in the cities, to be an urban nomad' (Deleuze and Guattari, 1988: 482). Being an urban nomad may therefore be common in programmes and courses where both staff and students are offered opportunities to reposition themselves away from the city and move into the desert, if only for moments in time. The term 'learning spaces', then, is used as both an ideology, as a way of being in higher education, and as a means of practising as an academic. This is captured through Giroux and Giroux's perspective that:

> In opposition to the commodification, privatization and commercialization of everything educational, educators need to define higher education as a resource vital to the democratic and civic life of the nation. The challenge is thus for academics, cultural workers, students and labour organizers to join together and oppose the transformation of higher education into a commercial sphere . . . (Giroux and Giroux, 2004: 120)

Conclusion

The creation of learning spaces might be something that is a choice. Perhaps, too, it is a choice that requires discipline. Those who are successful at finding, creating and using such spaces have discovered how to use them best for themselves. Thus such individuals find diverse ways of creating learning spaces such as generating opportunities for debate and ensuring they have space for writing – even if this demands rescheduling the working day to guarantee such space. Perhaps, then, finding and generating learning spaces is about the creation of an academic identity, whether smooth or striated.

2

Creating Learning Spaces

This chapter explores ways it might be possible to create learning spaces, not only in terms of the creation of personal learning spaces but also in terms of our understandings of the nature of higher education and the purpose of a university. This chapter explores work that set up challenges to institutional structures and assumptions, in order to suggest ways in which 'the university' can begin to create new forms of learning spaces. It argues for the importance of embracing troublesome knowledge and liquid learning, and suggests ways in which disciplines can change and adapt their pedagogies in order to create learning spaces within curricula.

Learning, spaces and curriculum

While theories of learning have never been static, the distinction between and across the approaches – behavioural, cognitive, developmental and critical pedagogy – continues to be eroded. There is increasing focus in the twenty-first century on what and how students learn and on ways of creating learning environments to ensure that they learn effectively – although much of this remains contested ground. New models and theories of learning have emerged over the past decade which inform the concept of curriculum spaces. For example, the work of Trigwell et al. (1999) on teachers' conceptions of learning offers useful insights into the impact such conceptions have on student learning, as does earlier work which has gained recent popularity, such as Vygotsky's zone of current and proximal development (Vygotsky, 1978). Yet, the work of Meyer and Land (2006), Haggis (2004) and Meyer and Eley (2006) has been critical of studies into conceptions of teaching and approaches to learning. This recent body of work, along with shifts away from the certainty of learning styles towards more holistic conceptions of learner approaches, is important in developing the debate away from generalizations and cognitive foci towards understandings of learner and teacher identities.

The notion of what counts as curricular spaces is an important concern. Much of the discussion about what and how academics learn and progress through their career has centred on the work of those in academic development units. For example, Land (2004) has provided a useful exploration of understandings of educational development, particularly in relation to uses of discourse and power. Yet much of the discussion about 'learning' for academics concentrates on professional or academic development rather than learning spaces, which could be seen as related, but in some cases opposing concepts. For example, some forms of academic development are striated learning spaces that merely focus on outcomes, performativity or, even, just course attendance. Accordingly, academic development in striated spaces tends to focus on competence and coverage rather than criticality. While there are many forms of academic development that offer smooth learning space, it is the underlying philosophies and theories of learning that illustrate most effectively the subtext underlying the creation of particular learning spaces. For example, programmes that prevent contestation of what is on offer and limit the theories used to those such as deep and surface approaches to learning (Marton and Säljö, 1984) close down opportunities for seeing learning as troublesome, under-researched and over-theorized. An example of the latter might include the literature on reflection and reflective practice.

Contesting curricula design

Although there have been many texts, articles and discussions about the nature of the curriculum and of creative ways of managing curricula (for example, Moore and Young, 2001; Barnett and Coate, 2002; Stephenson, 2002), globally many curricula remain unimaginative, constrained and modular. The modular system in particular tends to fragment and striate learning, and in many cases prevents the creation of disjunction in the mind of the student. Modules result in a tidy system of learning, where content is boxed into easily managed components that are not to be meddled with. Although the emphases in recent years on the development of clear goals for learning and improving the quality of teaching have been important, the impact of modular systems has created an increasingly performative approach to learning. The growing use of objectives in the 1980s by educationalists, such as Piper, Cox and Ramsden (see, for example, Light and Cox, 2001), was a means of ensuring that it was understood what students were expected to learn. Aims focused on the general intentions of the teacher, objectives focused on what students were expected to learn. However, in recent years there has been a move away from such a broad interpretation of behavioural models of curriculum design. In the late 1990s it became more common to design curricula around narrow constructions of content coverage and competence, and latterly there has been a move towards 'outcomes'. Furthermore, the work of Biggs (1999), who argued for constructive alignment, has tended to oversimplify the complex relationship between learning and assessment. While Biggs's ideas are useful for those new to teaching, his curricular constructions have become conflated and overused, resulting in the medium becoming the message. Such performative practices close down opportunities for creative curriculum design and structures, and prevent the development of curriculum spaces.

Yet to suggest the possibility of moving away from outcomes, objectives and 'covering content' appears to cause many staff distress and fear. This is not only because it is perceived as being pedagogically risky but also to do so would mean to challenge policy and funding directives which have insisted on these ways of operating. This might be partly related to the safety implicit in behavioural objectives, but it is also because to analyse the notion of behavioural forms of curriculum design is increasingly unusual in higher education, because of the loss of dialogic and reflective spaces. Further, partnerships with business, industry, not-for-profit organizations and the health services can often give rise to curricula designed according to what the 'customer' or purchaser believes they require. Yet I would argue that to embrace liquid learning and create smooth spaces, curricula need to be designed in ways that introduce questions about practices and understandings of knowledge within and beyond disciplinary areas, rather than just maintaining the status quo or even continuing to support hegemonic practices.

However, if the use of Bloom's (1956) taxonomy and the implementation of behavioural objectives are to be challenged there needs to be a viable alternative. The latter stance towards curriculum design has pervaded most systems of higher education worldwide, and this has meant not only performativity but also large-scale discounting of disciplinary differences and discipline-based pedagogies – which seem to have endured despite the demands of behavioural curricular design. It would seem then, rather than adopting a notion of curriculum whereby standardized designs are used for all disciplines, that instead curricula should be designed with troublesome knowledge as the centre point and not the counter point. Although it could be argued, in the UK at least, that such creative curricula do exist, it would seem that they are located either in the shadowlands or not presented as transparently as they might be, in order to avoid the scrutiny of those from the behavioural end of the quality assurance camp.

There has been increasing discussion about discipline-based pedagogy in the UK, particularly in the debates about the relationship between research and teaching. Jenkins and Zetter (2003) argue that disciplines shape the nature of pedagogy and such pedagogies reflect the practices and culture of the discipline. Consequently, teacher knowledge and beliefs about what to do, how to do it and under which circumstances, can affect the way that students learn particular subject matter. Shulman's work in the USA (1986; 1987) provides a framework for understanding teacher knowledge, in which he describes several layers that include both subject knowledge and pedagogical knowledge. Subject or content knowledge comprises the theories, principles and concepts of a particular discipline. In addition to this subject-matter knowledge, general pedagogical knowledge or knowledge about teaching itself is another important aspect of teacher knowledge. While subject knowledge and pedagogical knowledge are perhaps self-evident, Shulman (1986: 6) asks: 'why this sharp distinction between content and pedagogical process?' Somewhere between subject-matter knowledge and pedagogical knowledge sits discipline-based pedagogy. Shulman terms this 'pedagogical content knowledge', which he describes as:

> the ways of representing and formulating the subject that make it com-prehensible to others . . . Pedagogical content knowledge also includes an understanding of what makes the learning of specific topics easy or difficult: the conceptions and preconceptions that students of different ages and backgrounds bring with them to the learning of those most frequently taught topics and lessons. (Shulman, 1986: 9–10)

Yet standardized curriculum models, university programme boards and aca-demics who fail to understand educational curriculum design continue to overlook discipline-based pedagogy, and therefore particular kinds of fluid and open learning spaces within curricula are being lost.

Learning curricula and liquid learning?

A starting point for creating new curricula and new learning spaces might be to begin from the position that students need to develop problem-solving and problem management for an uncertain world. The difficulty with cur-ricula that focus on covering content is that by the time most students com-plete their undergraduate programme much of the knowledge learned will have changed and will have relatively little use value. Utilizing approaches to learning such as problem-based learning, project-based learning and action learning, approaches that enable students to see knowledge as being changeable and uncertain, will equip them to be independent inquirers who know how to find knowledge and develop capabilities for working in a shifting and uncertain world. Students do not need to learn through the imposition of outcomes and outputs, but instead through the development of an understanding of knowledge as a liquid, contestable concept. The issue of learning for an unknown future, as Barnett has suggested (1997), might seem to imply that disciplines are dead (or are soon to be so). Yet where does this leave discipline-based pedagogy and pedagogical content knowledge? How are curricula to be formed for and with uncertainty, but located in some form of disciplinary framework? Barnett (1997) suggested that designing curricula is a question of continual learning and understanding, but his arguments are dislocated from any sense of disciplinary relationship. Perhaps the application of Barnett's notion might be put into practice through shaping disciplinary knowledge in ways that create uncertain spaces, such as creating disjunction in the mind of the learner, adopting teaching

approaches that engage with critical contestability and recognizing in curricula proposals the uncertainty of knowledge. To adopt such approaches
will prepare staff and students for an unknown future while still accepting
that the nature and presence of a discipline does have an impact on learning.
The disciplines and their various pedagogies will not, I suggest, disappear
quite as readily as Barnett suggests. It might even be the case that discipline-
based pedagogy is bolstered and becomes stronger as the uncertainties about
what counts as knowledge grow.

In terms of curriculum design, uncertain curricula with liquid learning at
their centre would mean that a shift is required away from behavioural
models towards more humanistic models of learning and intentional curriculum frameworks. Liquid learning is characterized by emancipation,
reflexivity and flexibility, so that knowledge and knowledge boundaries are
contestable and always on the move. This kind of learning tends to occur in
action learning sets, creative project groups and some forms of problem-based
and scenario-based learning.

However, what is important about liquid learning is that it is constantly
changing. Liquid frameworks are ones through which staff pass on the way to
developing the pedagogical aims, in terms of the learning 'intentions' of the
course. Such transformative spaces are often 'liquid' in nature, so perhaps
the learning in such spaces should be termed 'liquid learning'. Hence,
rather than the current system of a series of distantly related modules, it
might be more effective to centre the curriculum on uncertainty and liquidity rather than content. Therefore, liquid learning would focus on diverse
forms of problem scenarios that could be taken in any order, or be sequenced,
but the focus would be on the problem-orientatedness of knowledge rather
than a notion of solid content. The current forms of ordering and containment inherent in current curricula seem to reflect a more modern than
postmodern stance to learning, of perhaps 'solid modernity'.

Bauman (2000) suggested that in the age of solid modernity, before the
1960s, there was a sense that accidents and sudden or surprising events were
seen as temporary irritants, since it was still possible to achieve a fully rational
perfect world. Solid modernity was characterized by slow change, where
structures were seen as being tough and unbreakable. Bauman has argued
that we have moved into liquid modernity, an era characterized by the social
and technological changes that occurred since the 1960s, embodied by
the sense of living in constant change, ambivalence and uncertainty. However, what is important here is that teachers consider their own roles and
pedagogical stance in this process, so that they recognize their own pedagogical values and beliefs about what counts as learning, curriculum and
what they bring to the learning context. Therefore, in such curricula, what
students learn is somewhat unpredictable and the view is taken that knowledge is seen as being constructed by the students in relation to the pedagogical aims of the teacher. Notions of both knowledge and curriculum
therefore become contested ground and both staff and students evaluate
personal knowledge and modes of knowledge in the process of curriculum

construction. Curriculum construction is therefore an active, interrupted and liquid process. However, depending on the discipline-based pedagogy, it may be important to make the distinction between training, instruction, initiation and induction. Stenhouse (1975) distinguished between these:

- Training is seen as the acquisition of skills, with the result that successful training is deemed as the capacity for performance.
- Instruction is concerned with the learning of information, so that successful instruction results in retention of information, such as a recipe for making chocolate cake.
- Initiation involves becoming familiar with social values and norms, so that successful initiation would be seen as the ability not only to interpret the social environment but also to anticipate the reactions to one's actions within it.
- Induction involves the introduction of someone into the thought system of the culture and here successful induction would be characterized by a person's ability to develop relationships and judgements in relation to that culture – induction for some people would also be seen as education – in its broadest sense.

Stenhouse (1975) suggested that the objectives model of designing curricula fits well with training and with instruction, but did not deal with the issues of initiation, because he argued that it tended to take place as part of a by-product of living in a community, such as an English public school. However, in the current climate, it would seem that initiation is very much part of the process of professional education, and thus initiation is a component of undergraduate professional education. Although Stenhouse has suggested that the main problem in applying the objectives model lies in the area of induction, it would seem that initiation is also important here. The issue then is how it is possible to develop curricula that allow for the moral initiation of students into the culture of the profession or discipline, while also inducting them into knowledge in ways that avoid indoctrination and promote democracy, creativity and working at the boundaries of disciplinary knowledge. Each of these types of curriculum model is likely to be more evident in some disciplines than others and in some universities than others, as delineated in, for example, Table 2.1. Training and initiation may be more likely to be located in an enterprise university, but that is not to say that engaging with uncertainty and contestable knowledge may not be part of such a curriculum.

However, one of the central difficulties of moving away from a modular system is the loss of flexibility for students learning about a given area over a short period of time. For example, part-time students studying in the evening are likely to choose one module and pause before the next. Rather than a series of optional distantly related modules, it might be more effective to centre the curriculum on uncertainty and liquidity rather than content. Liquid learning would focus on diverse forms of problem scenarios that could be taken in any order, or be sequenced, but the focus would be on the

Table 2.1 Curriculum models

Curriculum model	Disciplinary example	University type (based on McNay, 1995)	Curriculum focus
Training	Nursing Physiotherapy	Enterprise or Corporation	Competence Clients Loyalty
Instruction	Golf Computing	Enterprise	Customer Market Task
Initiation	Medicine Law Theology	Bureaucracy	Rules Regulation Rationality
Induction	Philosophy Politics English	Collegium	Consensus Discipline Freedom

problem-orientatedness of knowledge rather than a notion of solid content. To date, there has been little research exploring the impact of different types of problems on students' experiences of learning, nor has there been much exploration of the use of diverse types of problem at different levels of the course. Schmidt and Moust (2000) have argued that students acquire different categories of knowledge during their course of study and that diverse problem types will guide students towards these different categories.

The way in which questions are asked of students guide the types of knowledge with which they engage. For example, the question 'What is the matter with this man?' results in students seeking explanatory knowledge; knowledge that offers some reason for the symptoms the man is experiencing. Whereas if the students were asked, 'What would you do if you were this man's physiotherapist?' then the emphasis becomes one of action rather than explanation. The assumption is that the student always understands the explanatory knowledge and can take action, thereby using procedural knowledge. Such a distinction is important because it helps students to begin to understand how they recognize and use different types of knowledge. By enabling students to understand the differences between objective knowledge, personal knowledge and procedural knowledge, they will develop criticality through being enabled to engage with troublesome knowledge. If, for example, students understand that personal knowledge, representing people's attitudes and values, is more difficult to critique than objective knowledge, this will help them to see both the importance and challenges of their own moral perspectives on issues.

By focusing on explanatory knowledge new students can learn how to manage the knowledge associated with explanatory problems and fact-finding problems. Later in the course strategy problems are included. Finally complex moral problems can be introduced, along with other types of problems, as delineated in Table 2.2, making it possible to develop students towards criticality. Furthermore, problems could also be of different lengths, types and be increasingly messy as the programme progresses, but instead of students engaging with several problems simultaneously they would engage with only one at a time and links and overlaps would be assured between consecutive problems. Also, in the later part of the programme, students would be able to meddle with the problems on offer, thus creating the possible option of wiki and bliki (combination of a weblog and a wiki) style problems.

The curriculum itself would be contestable and the assessment negotiable. While such curricula would be seen by many as high risk, as long as robust assessment procedures are used that match the learning there is relatively little risk of students being a danger to themselves and others. Further, this form of curriculum creation can also encourage students to contest knowledge and the relative status of diverse knowledges. What is needed instead is a constructivist curriculum in which students can be active, social and creative learners. This is 'artful constructivism' Perkins (2006a) – the ability of teachers to shift and change, to be creative and notice troubles so that the learning context can be managed according to differences between learners.

Table 2.2 Creating learning spaces

	Curriculum focus	*Activities*			
Year 1	From problem-solving to problem finding	Explanatory problems	Fact-finding problems		
Year 2	From problem design to design specification	Strategy problems	Explanatory problems	Fact-finding problems	
Year 3	From wrestling with concepts to creativity and discovery	Moral dilemma problems	Fact-finding problems	Explanatory problems	Strategy problems

Learning spaces and knowledge status

Invariably the status of knowledge is contextual and thus knowledge is privileged in various ways in different contexts. However, it is increasingly the case that media knowledge has grown in importance to society in general. As a whole, there appears to be less cynicism and criticality about what is portrayed through mass communication than in former years. For example, Ross (2005) has argued that there is a problematic relationship between women and news media, in terms of their experiences, status and as subjects and sources of news stories. Even in the twenty-first century, higher education has remained a largely male space, with masculine value systems reflecting notions of knowledge, excellence and quality dominating the system. The result is not only that women tend to be given more administrative tasks and higher teaching loads, but also that their perspectives largely remain in silent spaces (see, for example, Ross and Carter, 2004). Whether it is because of media portrayal, lack of women in senior management or the struggle women have in locating themselves in male spaces, the dominance of men both numerically and positionally will no doubt continue to affect the forms of knowledge deemed to be acceptable in higher education. The increased power of the media in the way knowledge is portrayed and managed has affected the status of different forms of knowledge. As Lyotard remarked, 'knowledge and power are simply two sides of the same questions: who decides what is knowledge, and who knows what needs to be decided? In the computer age, the question of knowledge is now more than ever a question of government' (Lyotard, 1979).

The difficulty, then, is what is to be done about this in the university. The current state of play seems to be that it is the disciplinary areas that define the boundaries of knowledge within their disciplines. Yet this may differ from university to university and country to country, while at the same time the notion of disciplinarity is also breaking down. Furthermore, Bernstein (1996) has suggested that power and control are embedded empirically within one another while still being different. Power relations are seen as creating and legitimizing boundaries between categories and therefore always operate to produce dislocations, whereas control establishes legitimate forms of communication appropriate to the different categories. It would seem, then, that induction into a discipline is a power mechanism. The problematization of situations, by the creation and use of empowering problem scenarios, is a mechanism of control that *allows* communication to be established both across disciplines and between the theorizing of the discipline and the realities of practice. Edwards (1997) has suggested that the exercise of power (as opposed to the notion of power relations Bernstein defined) can been seen as disciplinary and pastoral, which is a useful distinction in the context of boundary spaces. Disciplinary power is the process by which the state gains knowledge and understanding about the population in order to govern its people. Expert discourses about issues such as crime, madness and education are provided, and therefore disciplinary knowledge becomes associated with particular practices and the induction into a particular kind of disciplinary identity. Thus, in the academic community, staff will use disciplinary knowledge and power to guide (and possibly subjugate) students into the discipline and encourage them to develop the appropriate disciplinary identity.

As knowledge, disciplines and knowledge of the disciplines fall about our ears, it seems that academics are increasingly turning away from some kind of utopian notion of defined forms of knowledge. Instead they are turning, and being turned by, government and industry towards the use value of knowledge. This idea, first developed largely by Lyotard, is one that has been taken up by a number of writers; Barnett (2003) in particular has argued against this and suggested instead that students need to learn for an unknown future. Yet this notion introduces questions about whether disciplinary knowledge has a place in Barnett's future.

Knowledge value and values

Knowledge status is also associated with the way in which knowledge, and which mode of knowledge, is valued and the way the underpinning values of a university affect the forms of knowledge that are esteemed and those that are not. This can be seen markedly in the difference between so-called teaching universities and research universities worldwide, where teaching (even in many teaching institutions) is seen as being of lower status than research. Yet the difficulty centres upon who decides what counts as knowledge in higher education. All too often tutors espouse that students are to be encouraged in the formulation of their own judgements, in challenging those of the academe and in evaluating the practice of the profession for which they are training. Yet although at one level tutors may offer such encouragement and sometimes support students in this process, all too often students adopt or revert to the developments of identities and strategies that will affirm academic and professional agenda. Assessment mechanisms, covert agenda and shifts to so-called efficiency in learning can all teach students to read the academe as a forum in which the ultimate goal is to beat the system.

A pertinent instance of this is the way in which knowledge, particularly in digital spaces, is seen as uncertain and troublesome, and more often for the lecturer than the students. For example, lecturers often criticize students for using wikipedia as a knowledge source, arguing instead that peer-reviewed journals are the only real sources of valid and reliable knowledge. Although some staff would argue that to take such a stance is to engage with values related to knowledge production, the subtext of such arguments would seem to be more about what is deemed acceptable knowledge within the academy and what it not. Wikipedia sits at the boundary space of acceptable and unacceptable knowledge, and students need to be enthused to engage with questions about knowledges and boundaries. Students should be encouraged to develop themselves, to learn to decide for themselves what counts as knowledge, to know how to defend their position and to be able to see valid knowledge as responsible knowledge rather than necessarily published knowledge. If staff are able to achieve this it will help to cultivate learners who will both challenge and enhance the interrelated worlds of theory and practice, as well as engage with the spaces in between.

At the same time, many institutions have developed codes of conduct as guidelines in an attempt to prescribe the actions of their employees. In our increasingly service-oriented economy, sound personal relationships based on proper conduct and high standards of ethical behaviour are invariably seen to be critical to long-term success. Further, values are now discussed increasingly in higher education, possibly because the breaking down of boundaries in our increasingly liquid society has meant that the whole idea of values is on the move. While, as Macfarlane (2005) points out, there is the need to re-engage with the notion of values and citizenship in higher education, I would suggest there is a danger that such re-engagement can also become performative, resulting in subjugation and control. Therefore, in order to engage with new spaces of knowledge creation and reformulation, it is vital that we engage with different curriculum spaces.

Creating curricular spaces

In order to create different learning spaces, spaces for an unknown future in which disciplinary difference and changing identities can be acknowledged, curricula, pedagogy and knowledge need to be explored and (re)presented in different and diverse ways.

Spaces for meddling with

Instead of curricula being over-planned, over-organized and over-prepared spaces, they should be spaces for meddling with. A starting point might be to do as McCarron (2006) has suggested and not provide students with bibliographies. McCarron argues that omitting bibliographies prevents us from directing students in a particular direction and encourages students to work out for themselves what they need to read for their assignment. So students will need to search library and electronic resources for themselves, thereby discovering the kinds of material available that relate perhaps not just to their subject, but perhaps more importantly to their own interests. However, if we are to create learning spaces where learning is liquid and knowledge is on the move, then curricula cannot be formulated in advance, as McWilliam has argued: 'the nature and purposes of *what counts as preparation must change*. From fixed and immutable, curriculum need to be conceptualised as *content for meddling with*. And this means a significant shift in what many teachers prioritise in their teaching' (McWilliam, 2005: 13, original emphases).

To shift curricula towards *intention* of learning and to stop trapping students into learning (as Biggs, 1999, has suggested) may feel high risk, but then risk is just what is missing. Higher education has increasingly become risk averse and so there is relatively little to meddle with. To create challenging curricular learning space requires that complexity, contestability and contradiction are central to learning and teaching.

Deliberative pedagogy

If we are to see curricula as content for meddling with, then we also need to see pedagogy differently. While there have been many quips about the new language of higher education, such as higher education or education for hire, or Falk's (1999) suggestion questioning whether it is lifelong learning or sentencing learners to life, there is a sense that academics are particularly good at writing about pedagogical difficulties (for example, Barnett, 2003; McWilliam, 2004, 2005). Yet there are few authors who offer strategies for dealing with negative performative practices upheld by constructive alignment and narrowly defined learning outcomes. Perhaps what is needed is more 'deliberative pedagogy' where deliberation rather than outcomes is seen as the organizing principle of the curriculum. This would mean that epistemic values, consensus decision-making, consciousness-raising and knowledge creation were the responsibilities of both learners and teachers, and deliberation was the hallmark of the curriculum rather than predictability.

Stolen knowledge

If we are to engage with deliberative pedagogy and unfinished curricula, it is important that we also value 'stolen knowledge': 'A very great musician came and stayed in [our] house. He made one big mistake . . . (he) determined to teach me music, and consequently no learning took place. Nevertheless, I did casually pick up from him a certain amount of stolen knowledge' (Rabindrath Tagore, quoted in Bandyopadhyay, 1989: 45). With the rise and diversity of work-based and work place learning, understandings of knowledge have changed and knowledge has been reformulated away from merely Mode 1 and Mode 2 knowledge (Gibbons et al., 1994). Mode 1 knowledge is propositional knowledge that is produced within academe separate from its use; the academy is considered the traditional environment for the generation of Mode 1 knowledge. Whereas Mode 2 knowledge is knowledge that transcends disciplines and is produced in, and validated through, the world of work (this is discussed further in Chapter 7). However, conceptions of knowledge and the management of knowledge in higher education largely remain ratified through traditional qualifications. Deliberative pedagogy and unfinished curricula necessitates knowledge being 'unpacked' so that living in, for and through work as well as the university are recognized as places in which knowledge can be 'stolen', claimed and examined in ways that can equip people for an uncertain and liquid world.

Conclusion

Creating learning spaces means re-engagement with our understandings and presuppositions of what counts as knowledge, curriculum and pedagogy. However, the creating of learning spaces also requires that we locate or re-view learning spaces and our identities within them. The next section of this book explores some of the learning spaces within higher education and challenges us to engage with them, deconstruct them, and engage with them 'differently'.

Part 2

Engaging Possibilities

3

Writing Spaces

Introduction

This chapter begins by discussing the importance of writing spaces. While there is a large body of academics that can and do already write copious amounts, there has been little in-depth discussion about how academics become successful publishers or how they develop spaces in which to write. This chapter discusses ways of not only creating writing spaces, but also of supporting staff to learn to speak for themselves and to create a 'writing voice'. It explores the ways in which staff develop the confidence and sense of personal authority and legitimacy to write and examine what it means to become a successful writer. However, it also introduces questions about writing practices and assumptions in relation to the New Literacy Studies movement. The section on the latter explores the interrelationship of writing, voice and multimodal writing spaces, and ways of representing ourselves in diverse textual modes.

A question of writing?

My interest in writing and the development of writing spaces emerged from concerns about why some academics write and publish and others do not. While some academics might argue that it is all a question of time, the issues would seem to be more complex that this. Writing up a thesis is often a large writing challenge and for many this is the space in which they learn to write and develop an academic voice. Yet, as academic tradition dictates, the textual voice of a thesis must not be too strident; there must be a sense of humility in the writing, since one is not yet deemed to have 'arrived'. Having gained entry to the doctoral world it was in fact the encouragement of an already experienced writer who prompted me to publish my first book. Remarks such as 'it is your duty to publish this' and 'academics must profess their profession' are words that still remain 'sound sounds' (Phipps, 2005: 12). It was in this book that I began to realize not only that I had something to say, but also that I could write in a particular style that has become what I define now as my 'writing voice'. Yet years later I was still puzzled by several questions:

- Why is it that some people write and others do not?
- How do academics approach writing?
- How do people *find* their writing voice?
- How are voices used differently for different purposes?
- Is writing planned or is it a question of finding flow . . . or both?

These questions are ones to which I return constantly, and yet it seems that many of the solutions lie in our biographies and identities. To some extent identity in academic life is forever problematic because it is always on the move, and in this sense writing is necessarily always a transitional process. However, it is noticeable that professional identities often seem to get in the way of writing. Many staff argue, 'well I am a physiotherapist, not an academic'. This oppositional self-definition, this sense of locating ourselves as someone that we are 'not', is invariably a barrier to writing.

Identity and voice

The beginning of writing for many staff originates in understanding how to position themselves within the academic community, of developing a location, a space and a stance from which to write. Writing tends to begin with our narrative view of other people's work, our perspectives on academic life, and it reflects our values and beliefs about what is important in academe. Yet the values many of us hold, or perhaps hold silently as we are restrained by new managerialism, are being moved backstage by the whispers that the views about liberal education and spaces to write are not considered sounds that should be heard. As we realize that writing is deeply connected to our identity, the challenges as to why some people are 'voiceless' and others are not become apparent. Initially it might seem that voicelessness in writing can be related to gender, to a woman's inability to speak and to often feeling 'silenced' by men and institutional politics; certainly the work of Belenky et al. (1986) would seem to suggest this.

An alternative view is that writing is *just* a question of practice and discipline, and although there are truths in such perceptions it is certainly more complex than this. For example, it is possible to turn to numerous books and articles that discuss how to write, what to do, how to structure the writing, when to write, and so on. Yet at the heart of writing there seems to be an element of personal risk. Perhaps this occurs in the necessity of challenging oneself, of developing a stance, of putting an opinion out there and being prepared to risk the hanging out of our identity in the public sphere where others can deconstruct it. It might be that this is why so many people avoid creating writing spaces and why academics' lives necessarily become filled with other business, because it is less risky, less costly and something over which there is more control.

Writing spaces and New Literacy Studies

In recent years there has been increasing interest in academic writing in the UK, although this is an area that is well established in the USA. Academic writing largely focuses on ways of writing and writing ways within particular disciplines, with an emphasis on mechanisms to improve writing, particularly for undergraduate students. Within the field of academic writing there is also a concern with issues of rhetoric and representation which seek to examine the ways in which disciplines, and academics in particular, choose to use text and media in specific ways. In a similar fashion to the emerging discipline of academic writing are the increasing number of texts that offer helpful guidance 'on' writing, whether for journals, essays or theses (for example, Philips and Pugh, 1987; Crème and Lea, 1997; Murray, 2005). These texts offer essential principles on how to manage time, and develop and use structures, as well as developing useful writing habits. There has also been considerable discussion about writing in the disciplines in the USA and, again like academic writing, is an area that has become of increasing concern in the UK, with the emergence of discussion about discipline-based pedagogy. Further, what is dwelt on by few writers is the sheer difficulty inherent in writing itself, in the complexity of creating writing spaces and of the ways of developing a writer identity.

The New Literacy Studies movement (NLS) offers some helpful insights, since it has helped to move the focus away from what occurs in the minds of individuals towards the importance of understanding literacy in the context of interaction and social practice. The NLS has helped to introduce questions about literacy as well as a body of work that can be used to inform the complexity of writing and publishing in higher education. For example, the NLS comprises a number of movements and social turns (Gee, n.d.), some of which are summarized below from Gee's paper, and seem to offer some guidance on how we might come to understand the importance and development of writing spaces:

> *Cultural models theory* has argued that people make sense of their experiences by applying largely tacit 'theories' or 'cultural models' to them. These are embedded in texts and social practices and therefore they shape ways of talking and writing.

> *Interactional sociolinguistics* suggests that social and institutional order is the product of social interaction, which produces and reproduces that order, thus 'knowing' is a matter of 'knowing how to proceed' in specific social interactions.

Narrative studies take the stance that people make sense of their experiences of themselves and others through a process of emplotment and story construction, which support and are supported by social practices, rituals and texts.

Postmodernism has focused on the notion of discourses which are characterized by 'ways of talking and writing about, as well as acting with and toward people and things', such as what counts as being marginal or normal or deviant.

Modern sociology has stressed the ways in which human thinking, acting and interaction are simultaneously structured by institutional forces and, in turn, give a specific order (structure, shape) to institutions. Yet simultaneously it is not possible to assess whether social practices inform institutions or vice versa, so this results in continually interrelated reproduction and transformation.

Nonetheless, as Gee points out, what has been omitted from these informing theories and ideas is:

the person as agent, who utters (writes) the words with (conscious and unconscious) personal, social, cultural and political goals and purposes. Of course, in social turn theories, the person's deeds and body are part of the situation or context, but the person as an actor engaged in an effort to achieve purposes and goals is left out as an embarrassing residue of our pre-social days. Consider, for example, how many postmodernists talk about people ('subjects') not so much as authoring their words, but of their words authoring ('subjecting') them . . . The person disappears other than as a historical and discursive construct. (Gee, n.d.)

The notion of writing spaces is not acultural or apolitical and is clearly located in understandings of identity and the way in which language, concepts and symbols are integrated by the individual into something that reaches beyond patchwriting (or patchwork writing), defined in Chapter 6.

Creating writing spaces

Writing spaces are opportunities not only to write but to reconsider one's stances and ideas, yet such opportunities tend to be both demanding and challenging. Yet the difficulty with the idea of creating writing spaces and of just writing itself, is that there is often a sense that others know how to use these spaces and write better than we do. Other people are intrigued by the way in which someone else writes, and they want to know their tips, their strategies and their exit routes from being stuck. There seems to be an assumption that there are hints and tips about how to go about creating writing spaces or the task of writing itself; short cuts that help to avoid the struggle and the pain. Yet this is one of the main challenges of being in a writing space, it is a space that no one else can create or inhabit. As writing spaces are our own spaces they are places where we also have to deal with our own disjunctions, or what Woolf (1931: 58) terms her 'angel'. Disjunction is used here to refer to a sense of fragmentation of part of, or all of the self, characterized by frustration and confusion, and a loss of sense of self. This often results in anger, frustration, and a desire for clear guidance and often hints and tips about how to move forward. For each of us there are issues that prevent us from writing.

Some people might refer to these as writing block, but this to some extent denies the nature of the disjunction; the sense of being stuck in writing. This is because the concept of a writing block is somewhat dislocated from ourselves; it is as if someone else has put the block there and the blame for the block is decentred. The idea of writing blocks is therefore not always helpful because it tends to suggest that there are kinds of block that are commonly experienced by many authors: tiredness, high workload, too many ideas, not enough ideas, nowhere to write, too many interruptions. While these are all important difficulties that have to be managed in order to create writing spaces, they are not the whole story. For example, during writing workshops participants are asked to list what it is that stops them from writing. The answers invariably are 'time, workload and unsupportive partner' but when people are encouraged to consider this question in more depth they begin to realize that the disjunction, the being stuck, is not disembodied or decentred, it is located in their identity and in the concerns that prevent them from writing. Writing, too, is a lonely occupation. It is relatively easy to discuss and debate our ideas, but it is often more difficult to portray them cogently in inked text. However, a helpful example is provided by Woolf (1931) who described this disjunction being located within herself. Here Woolf describes her 'angel', the phenomenon that appeared to constantly prevent her from writing:

> She was intensely sympathetic. She was immensely charming. She was utterly unselfish. She excelled in the difficult areas of family life. She sacrificed herself daily. If there was a chicken she took the leg; if there was a draught she sat in it – in short she was so constituted that she never had a mind or a wish of her own, but preferred to sympathize always with the minds and wishes of others. And when I came to write I encountered her with the very first words. The shadow of her wings fell on my page . . . (Woolf, 1931: 58)

There is an argument here suggesting that the angel is representative of the gendered nature of writing that occurred when Woolf was an author, in the sense that as a woman she was expected to do more important things than write. For Woolf it is clear here that the external constraints on her life and her gender are an issue, which is the case for many women in higher education in the early 2000s. What is particularly important about Woolf's stance is the sense of acknowledging her self as almost a sacrificial victim, that it was she who was both hunter and prey. She was a martyr because her sense of duty to others was rooted in a belief that she was necessarily less important than others. This exemplifies what often occurs in academic life, where the sense of the greater good, the sense of duty to the institution, the belief that teaching and administration are vital, overwhelm writing spaces so that opportunities to write are increasingly seen as privileged rather than *necessary* locations. Further, we often use blaming techniques in order to argue for how we have positioned ourselves and as the reason for not writing, this notion that we must undertake other things first and write last. Yet it is a responsibility, our responsibility to write; it is not the responsibility of anyone else and the difficulties and struggles are our own disjunction and must be owned.

However, when one is writing, and writing well, nothing else seems as important. There is a sense of 'finding flow' (Csikszentmihalyi, 1996) which is discussed later in this chapter, a sense that the writing flows onto the page – and certainly for many people there appears to be an inner knowledge, a sense that one must and can write immediately. Again, Woolf offers a poignant example:

> The one day walking around Tavistock Square I made up, as I sometimes make up my books, *To the Lighthouse*, in a great, apparently involuntary rush. One thing burst into another. Blowing bubbles out of a pipe gives the feeling of the rapid crowd of ideas and scenes which blew out of my mind, so that my lips seemed syllabling of their own accord as I walked. What blew the bubbles? Why then? I have no notion. But I wrote the book very quickly . . . (Woolf, 1940: 92)

While this experience may have happened to few of us, being a time when a sense of flow emerges spontaneously, there are other times when flow occurs as we are already in the process of writing.

However, there have been discussions and suggestions about 'types' of writers by authors such as Philips and Pugh (1987). Such suggestions largely draw on the work of cognitive psychologists who suggest that there are holist and serialist learners. Cognitive theories are directly concerned with mental processes (which include insight, information processing, memory and perception) rather than products (behaviour). Promoters of the cognitive tradition, including Tolman (1948), Piaget (1929) and Ausubel et al. (1978), have argued that new information has to be interpreted in terms of both prior knowledge and shared perspectives. The existing cognitive structure is therefore the principal factor influencing meaningful learning. In practice this indicates that meaningful material can only be learned in relation to a previously learned background of relevant concepts and hence the argument might be that we can only write in this vein too. To take this a step further might be to argue, following Pask (1976), that there are two general categories of a writing approach which can be identified in cognitive tasks. The holist writers identify the main parameters of a system and then fill in the details, while serialist writers progressively work through details to build up the complete picture as they go. Yet if writing is related to our identity and the difficulties stem from our own personal disjunctions then such an argument would seem naive. Further, such suggestions take little account of the changes in perceptions that occur over time.

For example, new writers tend to assume that by setting a day aside for writing that they will necessarily write during that time. Most experienced writers would argue that while a whole day is useful, indeed often vital at particular points in their writing, it is more important to develop and understand their own most effective personal writing habits. In contrast, other authors suggest that we should suspend our thinking, since thinking might hinder our writing. While this may be helpful for some people, again if writing is deeply connected to our identity and voice then it is perhaps more important to understand our own ebbs and flows of how and when we write best and what is likely to cause 'stuckness'.

Developing a voice and a writer identity

Creating writing spaces is not just about making time to write and finding a conducive atmosphere; finding ways of using such spaces is also important. Yet both the creation of space and the writing process relate to the development of voice and writer identity. For some academics writing becomes a passion, it is a place to stand, a place from which to speak, yet this is not the case for everyone. For many, writing and publishing has become an increasingly troublesome concern because of the necessary prerequisite of publishing copious amounts in order to ensure career development. However, even those who have published between three and five articles still find it difficult to write and to set out an argument in a coherent way. This would largely seem to be related to the lack of development of writer identity along with a sense of 'voicelessness' in the academic community.

Writer identity is defined here as the development of an ability to write that reflects our own stances, beliefs and values. It is not merely the reuse of other people's words and ideas, nor is it an article written in our words but littered with references and quotations from other sources. To have a writer identity is to speak in a voice that both reflects our individuality and locates our position within the academic community. Many of us have heard keynote speeches that have been full of the voices of others; when what we had come to hear was the speaker, we wanted to hear the speaker's 'take' and we did not want a crowd of other voices interrupting the speaker's voice. This need to locate, to position ourselves, is vital not only for the development of writer identity, but also in understanding the formulation of the academic text.

Boughey (2006) documents the struggles of students at a South African university whose life experience centred on oral traditions. The difficulties experienced by these students was evident in their inability to understand how to represent and locate themselves textually because in their home communities written texts were often authoritarian, but also tended to be set aside so that orality was privileged. The consequence was that students' authorial voices appeared to be unacademic, because they spoke with voices located in oral traditions and possessed a different understanding about the genres of academic written texts.

Many of us have read (and even written) articles that lack an argument and a sense of progression. In these there is little suggestion of what it is that the writer wants to convey and whatever suggestions are made tend to be bolstered with references and peppered with what 'better' academics have already said. Alternatively a lack of writer identity might emerge in arenas where there are formulaic ways of presenting material that must be followed in order that the research can be published. The consequence is that scientific results must be written and presented in a straightforward and unproblematic way, and because of the pre-existing formula relatively little is demanded of the writer. Yet other forms of writing require that we locate and position ourselves in relation to what we are writing. For example, a colleague who completed her PhD some years ago and possesses a substantial publication list explained that she still felt unable to take a stance and present her views publicly. This sense of voicelessness in writing is common. Further, there is a tendency for many academics to continue in this way and never really find a place to stand. This lack of writer identity, characterized by voicelessness, stems to some extent from the constant need to publish something, but largely from a lack of understanding about how to write, how to take a stance and the purpose of publishing in the first place. Silence also stems from our views, beliefs and cultural background about the value and purpose of texts. Developing a writer identity therefore requires:

- Taking a stance towards what is read
- Discovering and using a writing voice
- Finding flow
- Being prepared to take risks with ways of writing and presenting findings
- Understanding the circumstances when writing most easily takes place
- An appreciation of the importance of different writing strategies
- Recognizing that writing is a constant challenge to identity and is therefore necessarily troublesome
- Understanding that multimodal writing is complex.

Taking a stance towards what is read

For many of us, taking a verbal stance towards what we read is something that is not particularly difficult and it invariably produces good collegial debates. However, the ability to undertake this activity during the writing process and present a coherent argument and stance towards what is being argued for in a particular paper or text appears to cause disjunction. This may be related to the notion of voice development, but more often it appears to be connected to a fear of being unsure as to whether your stance towards the published work is brilliant or foolhardy. Moreover we are also afraid to take on, for example, Barnett (2003) because his is an illustrous text that has won prizes.

Yet it is only by beginning to see the faults and fractures in other people's work, by voicing our queries and by questioning their arguments that we can begin to make sense of, and then substantiate and write of, our own position. There is also often a sense that we do not 'know enough' to be able to take a stance and that this is ultimately linked to our sense of voice as a writer.

Discovering and using a writing voice

There often seems to be a sense of stuckness that occurs between the verbal and written voice: a colleague was a prime example of this; verbally she could argue, take up a stance and get her message across. Yet when she wrote she seemed to lose her voice and her ability to argue and position herself. She explained to me by email:

> I really found benefit following the last meeting we had . . . And won-
> dered if you had undertaken some 'special' psychotherapy training to
> employ with 'witterers' (or writers?) like me? Despite the 'lighthouse
> moments' that followed it has also left me with yet more perplexing
> locks to which, as yet, I have no key . . . Output in writing has amounted
> to nought . . . since I have continued verbalising more and more and
> being drowned in course review, marking, student support and teaching
> . . . Yours Sarah

The ability to develop a voice relates to our learner identity, not just our writer identity. Learner identity expresses the idea that the interaction of learner and learning, in whatever framework, formulates a particular kind of identity. The notion of learner identity moves beyond, but encapsulates, the notion of learning style, and encompasses positions which students take up in learning situations, whether consciously or unconsciously. For many academics new to writing there is a sense of not really knowing whether they have anything to say, a sense of not being worthy of saying anything. Furthermore, there is also a concern that what they want to say may have been said already by someone else – and more eloquently. Even if these barriers have been overcome, the next uncertainty that haunts the would-be writer is the question of whether anyone will listen, and if they do, will they laugh at the ideas and the argument?

Yet, 'learning to write' and 'learning to speak' is mentioned relatively little in academic circles. Research into student learning is helpful here, for example, students who engage with disjunction in a learning environment tend to speak of 'gaining a voice' (Savin-Baden, 2000), as a way to depict an intellectual and ethical process whereby the development of a sense of voice, mind and self are interlinked. Further, in research by Belenky et al. (1986), the ability to 'construct a voice' encompassed the way in which women spoke of the transitions that often ensued after being stuck. Accordingly I would suggest that the notion of constructing a voice is a dynamic process which changes and moves according to the context. For example, some writers can 'speak' in some contexts and not others, yet there is not always a conscious realization of voice (or lack of it). Yet the ability to understand voice construction as being a changing process can enable staff to articulate their own confusions around writing. This often results in a shift towards a greater consciousness and/or understanding of their writer identity, and a move towards finding flow.

Finding flow

The concept of finding flow in writing is based on the work of Csikszentmiha- lyi. Flow is that state of engagement in a skilful and challenging task, where time seems to fly by. The examples he has cited in particular are driving and mountaineering. In mountaineering and in particular rock climbing there is sense that the moves flow, with ease, grace and rhythm. Csikszentmihalyi defines flow as: 'being completely involved in an activity for its own sake. The ego falls away. Time flies. Every action, movement, and thought follows inevit- ably from the previous one, like playing jazz. Your whole being is involved, and you're using your skills to the utmost' (Csikszentmihalyi, 1996: 1).

Csikszentmihalyi has suggested people who have experienced flow con- sistently report the same seven dimensions of flow, which include:

- Completely involved, focused, concentrating – with this either due to innate curiosity or as the result of training
- Sense of ecstasy – of being outside everyday reality
- Great inner clarity – knowing what needs to be done and how well it is going
- Knowing the activity is doable – that the skills are adequate, and neither anxious or bored
- Sense of serenity – no worries about self, a feeling of growing beyond the boundaries of ego – afterwards a feeling of transcending ego in ways not thought possible
- Timeliness – thoroughly focused on present, do not notice time passing
- Intrinsic motivation – whatever produces 'flow' becomes its own reward.

Yet, authors in both the academic and the popular world often argue that they find, as Woolf mentioned earlier, that sometimes the writing 'just flows' unexpectedly. For many such writers it often seems that their ideas have been fermenting for some time and then they flow straight onto the page. How- ever, for others there is a belief that just by allowing the unconscious self to write, flow will occur (Bolton, 1999). This is an approach of 'don't think just write,' so that there is a sense of 'suspension of disbelief', therefore 'endeavours should be directed to persons and characters supernatural, or at least romantic, yet so as to transfer from our inward nature a human interest and a semblance of truth sufficient to procure for these shadows of imagin- ation that willing suspension of disbelief for the moment, which constitutes poetic faith' (Coleridge, [1817] 1983: 168–9).

What would seem to be most important in the writing process is recognizing the times when flow has occurred, possibly in another situation, but in particular when it does happen in writing, whether it is blogging, reflection or even writing an email.

Being prepared to take risks with ways of writing and presenting findings

While there are particular customs associated with writing textbooks, monographs and journal articles, the process of taking risks is a mechanism that can help the development of writer identity. For example, writing an article in the first person (which may not be acceptable to the given journal) introduces a number of questions. First, it prompts us to consider what we believe about using the first person. Second, it helps to consider and reconsider our perspective, because using 'I' helps us to position ourselves with the writing and in relation to the literature; we are no longer a disembodied third person. When writing in the first person it becomes possible to see one's own interpretations and personal stances. Third, it helps to question whether we want to write in a style that promotes disembodiment or whether we want to change tack and position our writing in a different space. Another alternative is to try different methodological approaches to research or to undertake some research that raises questions about the discipline itself which may interrupt disciplinary narratives.

Understanding the circumstances when writing most easily takes place

The creation of a writing space has to relate to one's own lifestyle and ways of working best. For some people this may mean the use of a writing retreat, a place without telephones and email, in a beautiful setting with someone to help to guide the writing process. For others writing in cafés or noisy rooms is a writing space. The creation of a writing space is neither straightforward nor easily delineated; it is something that relates very much to who we are as individuals. For me a writing space is somewhere quiet, with no music, with opportunities to walk, with beautiful views and as few opportunities as possible to talk to anyone about anything. Yet I have a colleague who positions her desk in the middle of the family living space where she can see the television and where she can write around the chaos of family life. However, it is not just the physical space that is important, the psychological circumstances are also important. For example, some people have a need to clear their mind of clutter while tidying a physical space in which to write. Some individuals prefer to trust the unconscious and just write, yet others write better in warm climates away from home where they can both physically and psychologically withdraw.

An appreciation of the importance of different writing strategies

While there are, as aforementioned, a number of texts that offer guidance about diverse writing strategies, it is important to note that trying different approaches can help to cultivate a sense of the kinds of activities that support the development of writer identity. For example, using a mentor, sharing ideas via email, belonging to a writing group, blogging, attending writing retreats and undertaking ten-minute writing slots can all be helpful approaches to develop a writer identity. Writing will then become a some-what less troublesome habit. However, it is important to note that writing strategies need to become part of the discipline of writing, writing needs to be seen as a choice, not as something for which we make excuses.

Recognizing that writing is a constant challenge to identity

In the process of the development of a writer identity it is important to realize that this identity is constantly on the move. Writing, like life, is never stable and, as such, it can be a troublesome process. For some academics, writing and becoming a writer is a constant source of disjunction; they always feel stuck, and this may relate to finding it difficult to know what to put on the blank white page. Yet for others there is a sense of thoughts always being jumbled, with little idea of what is important and what is not. Yet as writer identity begins to develop and emerge it also changes, and this can be troublesome because as we take a stance towards knowledge our perspectives shift. Such shifts can be challenging, because to question and critique con-stantly brings with it the realization that knowledge in itself is troublesome. Perkins (1999) has argued for four forms of troublesome knowledge, but believes that there might be other sources of troublesomeness in knowledge; these are summarized as follows:

- Ritual knowledge is where we do not really understand a concept but are able to do things by rote. Thus, 'Names and dates often are little more than ritual knowledge. So are routines in arithmetic ... such as the notorious "invert and multiply" to divide fractions.' (Perkins, 1999: 7)
- Inert knowledge 'sits in the mind's attic, unpacked only when specifically called for by a quiz or a direct prompt but otherwise gathering dust' (Perkins, 1999: 8). Therefore we might learn about concepts but not really relate them to our own life, such as learning about society but not being able to relate it to our own position in society.
- Conceptually difficult knowledge is a mix of misimpressions from every-day experience (objects slow down automatically), and reasonable but mistaken expectations (heavier objects fall faster).

- Alien knowledge is characterized by Perkins (1999: 10) as that which 'comes from a perspective that conflicts with our own'. For example, we may not understand issues that come from someone else's perspective or culture.

It would seem that both the development of a writer identity and the changing nature of such an identity is conceptually difficult knowledge and alien knowledge. This is because in the development of writer identity many people assume that writing is a gift and that it is easy to do with practice and experience, but there is little realization that writing is something to be continually understood and worked at. Further, for many academics the notion of a writer identity 'on the move' is somewhat alien. There is a sense that once success is achieved in publishing that this will always be the case, and the possibility that this and one's writer identity could shift would be seen as alien. However, the notion of troublesome knowledge bears further exploration and this is undertaken in Chapter 7.

Understanding that multimodal writing is complex and requires the use of different voices

Multimodal writing is defined here as the ability to write in different styles for distinct audiences using diverse media. There is often an assumption that writing for a newspaper or magazine is easier than writing a book or journal article; yet each medium brings different challenges. While for some people developing a writer identity may be seen as a 'threshold concept', the idea of a portal that opens up a way of thinking that was previously inaccessible (Meyer and Land, 2003a; 2003b; 2003c), the ability to write across different modes seems to demand the crossing of a threshold for each different mode. There are few writers who find it straightforward to practice multimodal writing because it demands a shift in writing style and use of voice.

However, multimodal writing has become increasingly complex following the introduction of screen-based technologies. Jewitt suggests that such technologies 'remediate reading and writing practices' (Jewitt, 2005: 316). What she argues is that the position and use of images on screen changes the relationship between image and writing, so that writing becomes decentred. Such changes in the use of images are beginning to change what reading and writing are. Yet it is interesting to note that electronic texts are mirroring print-based texts in terms of styles and representation, which would therefore seem to suggest that, despite Jewitt's argument, in higher education at least, print-based formats are still largely defining the nature of how reading and writing should be. However, as changes occur in forms and styles of reading and writing so the nature, purpose and use of writing spaces will, no doubt, transform as well.

Conclusion

To date much writing remains in print-based forms, yet academics author texts for digital spaces and this can be seen too as a writing space. However, the use of writing spaces of whatever kind is vital for the academic. Such spaces remain undervalued and underused. Understandings and uses of time and space have been changed by the introduction of the Internet, resulting in a sense of global borderlessness. Yet living and working without borders is not always helpful. We seem to be living in times of both performativity and borderlessness, but writing spaces are interstitial spaces that must be captured in order that neither borderlessness nor performativity eliminate such spaces.

4

Dialogic Spaces

Introduction

The notion of learning though dialogue is not new, but the notion of dialogic spaces is a concept that is presented and explored here. This chapter examines the importance of dialogue as a learning space, arguing that discussion is an important site for learning and the development of intellectual ideas and that dialogic critique is one such site that is increasingly overlooked by academics. It argues that the development of the critical being occurs though discussion and argument. Yet it is evident that colleagues often reflect on the lack of space in academic life for intellectual debate – but at the same time many seem to forget that it is part of the role and responsibility of an academic to find such spaces.

Locating dialogic spaces

Invariably when dialogue or dialogic learning is discussed in academic circles, there is an underlying assumption that dialogue necessarily involves conversation – that the focus is always oral. Yet dialogic spaces also encompass the complex relationship that occurs between oral and written and the way, in particular, that written communication is understood by the reader. Thus dialogic spaces transcend conceptions of dialogue, which is invariably conceived as the notions of exchange of ideas, and dialectic as the conception of transformation through contestability. This is because dialogic spaces encompass written and verbal communication with others and one's self, but also dialogic spaces have at their core the sense that through encountering and engaging with dialogic spaces (within which conflict and disjunction is likely) transformation will result. Although it might be suggested that dialogic spaces *necessarily* require or assume partnership or relationship, this in fact is not the case. It is argued here that dialogic spaces reach beyond the notion of authentic dialogue, as argued by Buber (1964), in which it is necessary to have an authentic relationship with another. This is because Buber's notions tend to centre on a perception of selfhood that is static, whereas Hall has argued:

> . . . identity does not signal that stable core of the self, unfolding from beginning to end through all the vicissitudes of history without change . . . Nor – if we translate this essentializing conception to the stage of cultural identity – is it that collective or true self hiding inside the many other, more superficial or artificially imposed 'selves' . . . identities are never unified, and in late modern times, increasingly fragmented; never singular, but multiply constructed across different . . . discourses, practices and positions. (Hall, 1996: 3–4)

Thus, it is argued here that what is needed instead is not a static view of self but a liquid view – a sense of multiple identities that shift and change with time.

However, changes in academic life, particularly in the early 2000s with the shift towards performative practices and accountability, have resulted in a reduction in dialogic spaces, and remarks heard around the campus reflect this. While it could be argued that academic life has always been fraught with busyness, the sense of space to discuss and debate seems to be one that is increasingly devalued. It is devalued not only through short agenda-led meetings but also through long rambling meetings that focus on planning rather than debating ideas and concepts. If as academics we are both to have the authority to teach and to take a stance on political and pedagogical issues, then we need to create dialogic spaces – spaces where contesting knowledge and political positions are at the forefront of debate, not at the bottom of the agenda.

The difficulty with neither recognizing nor engaging with such spaces is not only seen in the overvaluing of Mode 1 knowledge by both staff and students, but also in the shifts away from perceptions of responsibility and expectation in academic life. For example, students expect to be nurtured, told what to do, what to read and how to think. Rarely these days do lecturers challenge students to consider their position in the learning process or engage them in the process of taking a stance towards knowledge. This lack of expectation of students by staff is creating a culture of dependency within the university, which is compounded by staff's need to cover ground, create outcomes, define knowledge – which is a further barrier to students taking responsibility for their learning. A possible solution would be to adopt 'strategies of omission' (McCarron and Savin-Baden, 2007) in order to prevent the development of co-dependent relationships, over-engagement and collective cocooning. There are fours strategies of omission, all borrowed from stand-up comedy, which might be used. They are summarized here:

1. *Improvisation, rather than preparation*: getting rid of the 'lesson plan' and, like a compere, stay flexible enough to let students lead the discussion. Without a 'script', it is still possible, and actually it is extremely desirable, to have a very broad, yet perfectly sufficient, agenda.

2. *Detachment, rather than relationship*: relationships and rapport with students are not always 'the basis of best teaching', any more than they are to good comedy; indeed they may well be hostile to it.
3. *Challenge, rather than support*: seminars should not be 'cosy' or 'friendly;' on the contrary every now and then, students need to know how much they do not know, and how much, by a given stage at university, they should know. As a profession we are far too willing to believe that the learning experience should be 'pleasurable'.
4. *No names, rather than most names*: being able to learn the names of students needs to be seen as a congenial aspect of a very specific, historically and economically determined, learning and teaching environment; not as an indispensable, precondition for 'good teaching' (McCarron and Savin-Baden, 2007).

Yet the problem is twofold – staff also expect to be given knowledge. At a recent conference a delegate said he had been disappointed with the workshop he had chosen to attend, because he had wanted the expert to share all his views and knowledge. The session had been publicized as a workshop with debate and discussion as the central approaches to learning. Although the expert had written many books and papers which delineated his perspectives on the subject, the delegate still wanted to be *told* the information rather than to engage with arguments and explore the ideas presented. Thus it would seem that the issues of conception and purpose in learning spaces, particularly dialogic spaces, are often misconstrued. This introduces questions about the contradictions that arise between what is meant in written communication and what is understood. Such misconceptions are often neither noticed nor discussed. However, perhaps what is important here is not only the conception of the purpose of particular dialogic spaces, such as workshops, but the way in which the activities of a learning space are communicated to participants and translated by participants into something that is meaningful for them.

Forms of dialogic spaces

Dialogic spaces are therefore spaces in which critical conversations occur and ones where change and challenge take place. Dialogic spaces are not only those that are created on campus through meetings and research forums, they also need to be re-created at conferences. Too often conferences are packed with papers where the presenters speak for too long and opportunities for discussion are prevented. Those presenting keynote speeches often fail to challenge and provoke debate, and instead present a few pleasant thoughts for the day. Dialogic spaces for debate will only begin to re-emerge when the importance of such spaces is realized. However, dialogic spaces are not only those that occur in the cafés and at the end of meetings, instead they are formed and formulated through our positions and identities as academics. Such spaces are not those of idle chat but are where criticality and argument are centre stage and include the following varieties.

Dialogic learning

Dialogic learning (Mezirow, 1985) is learning that occurs when insights and understandings emerge through dialogue in a learning environment. It is a form of learning where staff and students draw upon their own experience to explain the concepts and ideas with which they are presented, and then use that experience to make sense for themselves and to explore further issues. The promotion of such forms of learning can encourage both staff and students to critique and challenge the structures and boundaries within higher education and industry, whether virtual or face to face. This is because learning through dialogue brings to the fore, for students and tutors, the value of prior experience to current learning and thus can engage them in explorations of and (re)constructions of learner identity. However, Flecha (2000) has developed the concept of dialogic learning further, suggesting seven principles which include egalitarian dialogue, the valuing of cultural intelligence and transformation. What is helpful about these principles is that they extend Mezirow's conception of dialogic learning, by embracing the work of Freire (1974) and encompassing Habermas's (1984) theory of communicative action. The focus, then, of this form of dialogic learning is in seeking to understand and engage with difference and complexity in the context of egalitarian and reasoned argument.

Dialogic reading

The concept of dialogic reading was developed in early years education but is useful here both as a means of helping students to develop their ideas, and particularly for staff to engage in dialogic spaces. Dialogic reading is 'the intersubjective process of reading and making meaning from text, in which readers strengthen their reading comprehension, deepen their literary interpretations and reflect critically about life and society thus opening up possibilities of personal and social transformation' (Soler and Racionero, 2004). Thus this form of reading relates not only to meaning-making but also to the collective understanding of those who are reading the text. Examples of dialogic reading would include journal clubs and reading groups. However, dialogic reading would focus beyond the mere discussion of the text and focus on understanding through the collective. The opportunity to engage with these kinds of spaces to discuss texts is tending to decrease with the information overload of texts, whether inked or virtual, of the early 2000s. Yet such spaces need to be formed and fashioned, so that collective dialogic learning and reading spaces can emerge.

Stories and narratives

What counts as 'story' varies within methodological and disciplinary fields. The biographical-interpretative method was first developed by German sociologists to produce accounts of the lives of holocaust survivors and Nazi soldiers (see, for example, Clandinin and Connelly, 1994, for more discussion on narrative approaches). This method is part of the narrative tradition and the main theoretical principle in this method is the idea that there is a gestalt, a whole that is more than the sum of its parts, informing each person's life. It is the job of the biographers to elicit this 'meaning frame' rather than follow their own concerns.

However, when using stories to create dialogic spaces it is important that staff are not only able to ask questions that elicit stories, but also that they are able to 'position' themselves so that stories can be analysed effectively. For example, some academics would argue that stories largely emerge from questions asked. However, there are those within the interpretive tradition who disagree with this stance, and would always ask participants to tell and define their story in a way that would convey the meaning that they, as participants, would wish to be heard. Stories constructed by the narrator (written, verbal and even, film) have been used by anthropologists and sociologists who label their work as ethnography. Yet the distinction between different types of stories tends to be in the co-construction and strategies for interpretation rather than between the traditions and disciplines. Despite this theorizing there is often a sense that stories are just something that are told to explain or make a point, whether within a lecture or a seminar, and it would be easy to assume that stories are merely subjective. Nevertheless, the whole notion of story-telling is more complex than is often supposed. For example, telling a story may be undertaken for a whole host of reasons; it may be told in a particular way using different sounds and voices, but also as a verifying mechanism, as a means of confirming or defending truths. Alternatively they can be used as a means of control. For example, in professional education, stories from practice can promote the idea that a given story represents what it means to be a 'good' nurse or an 'excellent' teacher. Thus, story-telling can be a means of laying claim to a particular notion of professionalism in order to encourage students to take up particular modes of practice. Stories are difficult to argue with when presented as good practice and therefore they are immediately problematic as representations of life. This is because stories are both connected to, and representative of, identities and thus to criticize a story is often interpreted as a criticism of identity.

Soliloquy as a dialogic space

For some authors, such as Buber (1964) and Bakhtin (1981; 1984), soliloquy is not seen as a place of dialogue. Bakhtin argues that monologism is not an authentic way of being, suggesting:

The single adequate form for *verbally expressing* authentic life is the *open-ended dialogue*. Life by its very nature is dialogic. To live means to partici-pate in dialogue: to ask questions, to heed, to respond, to agree, and so forth. In this dialogue a person participates wholly and throughout his whole life: with his eyes, lips, hands, soul, spirit, with his whole body and deeds. He invests his entire self in discourse, and this discourse enters into the dialogic fabric of human life, into the world symposium. Reified (materialising, objectified) images are profoundly inadequate for life and for discourse. (Bakhtin, 1984: 293, original emphases)

Bakhtin's argument stresses the importance of language as dialogue so that 'the word' is seen as two-sided because of its social use by speakers. However, it is argued here that soliloquy is an important discursive site in the context of dialogic spaces. This is because the concept of dialogic spaces does not preclude dialogue with one's own identities, since it is through soliloquy that individual meaning-making occurs. Thus, Hamlet, in deciding whether to murder his uncle, discusses with himself not only whether he has the courage to carry out the murder, but also the consequence of it in both earthly and heavenly realms:

> Now might I do it pat, now he is praying;
> And now I'll do't. And so he goes to heaven;
> And so am I revenged. That would be scann'd:
> A villain kills my father; and for that,
> I, his sole son, do this same villain send
> To heaven . . .
> To take him in the purging of his soul,
> When he is fit and season'd for his passage?
> No! (*Hamlet*, Act 3, Scene 3, Shakespeare, 1601)

The soliloquy then can be seen as not only a dialogic space but also a reflect-ive space, and for Hamlet this can been seen as a space where reflection and dialogue collide. His competing identities about the desire to revenge his father's death and the possibilities that open up if he kills his praying uncle, is a place of liminality and as he soliloquizes he comes to a position of realization. The dialogic space has enabled him to construct meaning and to doubt his intentions, and prompted him to remove himself and reflect fur-ther on the best position from which to act. Thus the notion of soliloquy as a dialogic space captures the idea that we have dialogic identities, identities that inform one another but may also compete with each other and cause conflict and disjunction in our lives.

Socratic dialogue

Dialogic spaces also include Socratic dialogue. Socrates believed that knowl-edge was unattainable and thus used dialogue and questioning approaches to probe student understanding of moral concepts such as justice, and applied formal logic to their ideas to show inconsistencies, inadequacies and weaknesses of their beliefs. 'The Socratic Method' was developed by Nelson in the 1920s. Its objective was to use collective reflection and introspection: 'the ultimate standards – logical, ethical, esthetic [*sic*] – that are implicit in our ordinary judgments' (Nelson, 1949: vi). Nelson's work has focused more on the development of group critique, reflection and decision-making, rather that the somewhat teacher dominated model espoused by Socrates. Thus Socratic dialogue of the twenty-first century would appear to focus more on the facilitation of questioning than the critique of the questions themselves. These dialogic spaces are designed to create a very open and collaborative environment for questioning and examining forms of knowledge, problem situations or areas of research, for example. The idea is that constructive inquiry is used to explore possible solutions, but also that the shortcomings of possible solutions are also explored in detail. Therefore these Socratic dialogic spaces are places in which, through discussion and sharing ideas, new understandings emerge and connections are made. Yet such spaces are also places where gaps are realised and uncertainty recognized. Although dialogic space might emerge in reflective spaces and digital spaces, it is more often 'seen' in the academic community in face-to-face meetings, where meaning construction occurs through discussion.

Online dialogic spaces

For a number of years there has been interest in, and attempts to understand, notions of embodiment in online dialogic spaces. Many of the questions raised by authors in the field centre on questions about 'presence' and the extent to which the body is dislocated when speaking online. For many people the silence of online dialogue is disconcerting, as is the turn-taking required in live chat sessions. However, one of the issues that seems to raise serious concerns is that of netiquette. The difficulties here stem from perceptions about how one should speak online and whether emoticons should or should not be used. While at one level some of these issues seem trite, there are strong views held about behaviours online in ways that are not voiced with regard to classroom settings. Further, the very fact that online dialogue is seen, moderated, maintained and recorded means that 'bad behaviour' can be printed off and used as evidence. It would seem that online spaces may begin to change the nature of dialogue, not only in such spaces but also in terms of how people choose to speak, communicate and be present face to face, but this will be discussed further in Chapter 6, 'Digital Spaces'.

While there are differences in online dialogue compared with face-to-face communication, there would also appear to be some interesting myths and assumptions. The idea that one's body is not present online is a myth that seems to prevail, and although the hands that work the keyboard may not be synchronous with the voice that speaks in textual form, the identities of that person are still present. There are some interesting differences in comparing online and face-to-face dialogue in terms of how one portrays oneself and whether, in fact, it is different. There are also those, such as Feenberg (1989), who have suggested that online communication is not tacit because we are unable to see and perhaps read participants' non-verbal communication. Yet there is a sense that it is possible to read signals in online communication, but because it is a relatively new form of dialogic space there is a tendency to overlay this textual communication with understandings and assumptions from face-to-face communication. Yet it would also be true to say that the lack of familiarity renders what is often seen as familiar – the reading of text and analysing subtext – as different and strange.

Disciplinary dialogues

Dialogic space within disciplines would seem to be spaces where academic identities and positions are formulated, made and managed. Thus, discipline-based pedagogy promotes and maintains the disciplinary status quo and the power plays within those disciplines. For example, Mills (2006) has argued that in order to launch and manage an academic career successfully it is important that future academics 'demonstrate and embody a "deep" Weberian commitment to their field and specialist research subject'. Thus mimicry and mastery of disciplinary rules are what constitute the underlying game of becoming a successful academic. Research on teacher knowledge has been common in secondary education for some time. Teacher knowledge and beliefs about what to do, how to do it and under which circumstances can affect the way that students learn a particular subject matter. Shulman's work (1986; 1987; 2005a; 2005b) provides a framework for understanding teacher knowledge in which he describes several layers that include both subject knowledge and pedagogical knowledge. Subject or content knowledge comprises the theories, principles and concepts of a particular discipline. In addition to this subject matter knowledge, general pedagogical knowledge or knowledge about teaching itself is an important aspect of teacher knowledge. This general pedagogical knowledge has been the focus of most of the research on teaching. While subject knowledge and pedagogical knowledge are perhaps self-evident, Shulman (1986: 6) asked, 'why this sharp distinction between content and pedagogical process?' Somewhere between subject-matter knowledge and pedagogical knowledge lies pedagogical-content knowledge. Pedagogical-content knowledge, he asserts, draws upon knowledge that is specific to teaching particular subject matter and he describes pedagogical-content knowledge as:

> the ways of representing and formulating the subject that make it comprehensible to others . . . Pedagogical content knowledge also includes an understanding of what makes the learning of specific topics easy or

difficult: the conceptions and preconceptions that students of different ages and backgrounds bring with them to the learning of those most frequently taught topics and lessons. (Shulman, 1986: 9–10)

Such a situation therefore introduces questions regarding Shulman's work (Shulman, 2005a; 2005b), since he chooses not to examine the relationship between pedagogical signatures and discipline-based pedagogies. For example, it might be the case that pedagogical signatures are identity-based and imprinted through discipline-based pedagogy. Thus in practice, both in teaching and in research, pedagogical signatures may in fact be individual interpretations of discipline-based pedagogy rather than the narrowly defined conception Shuman offers. Thus where there are clashes and difficulties when disciplines attempt to work at and across the boundaries of one another, difficulties emerge because of disciplinary blindness. Often it seems that individuals are unaware of, and unable to explain, the hidden rules and practices of the discipline in which they work, and do not always recognize or understand the problems associated with transgression. They know that transgression has occurred and has interrupted disciplinary narratives, but they often are unable to articulate the nature of the transgression to someone else in another discipline, because of hidden assumptions and invisible rules.

Reciprocal spaces

Although there is invariably a covert assumption in dialogic encounters that those speaking should respect one another and listen to each other's views, the actual practice of not only creating dialogic spaces but also ensuring that a sense of egalitarianism takes place within them is problematic. Habermas (1984) has argued for the presence of an 'ideal speech situation', idealized conditions of speech which focus on the notion of better argument. In the ideal speech situation, systematically distorted communication is excluded so that:

1. Participants of discourse have equal rights to use speech acts in ways that are always open to claims, argument and question.
2. Participants have equal opportunities to present their perspectives and their arguments.
3. Participants make their intentions apparent and express, equally, their views and wishes.
4. Participants have opportunities to order, resist orders, to promise and refuse, to be accountable and to demand accountability from others.

Thus for Habermas the ideal speech situation must not just be a theoretical construction, but must take into account veracity, comprehensibility, sincerity and appropriateness (Habermas, 1984: 306–8). Yet the changes in higher education in the twenty-first century are such that we have lost sight of the value of such validity claims. While equality will always be an ideal, as indeed will the ideal speech situation, perhaps what we should be plumping for is 'open dialogue'; a space where interrogation within and across disciplines can occur, and perhaps more importantly a space where the fabric of higher education can be deconstructed. Those engaged in such speech are members of a society in which their position, in terms of responsibility and autonomy, is reconsidered. Thus for Habermas the expectation of the dialogue is that it is non-authoritarian and therefore emerges from a position in which 'our modes of reciprocally constituted ego identity and our idea of true consensus are always implicitly derived' (Habermas, 1972: 314). However, issues of power, control, race, equality and gender in higher education would seem to point to Habermas's position being rather Panglossian in nature. To argue for a position of an ideal speech situation would seem to suggest that it is possible to achieve equality and reciprocity.

Those from the field of adult and community education would argue that this position is one to strive for, and indeed the work of Freire (1974) adopts a more political stance by exploring how deeply embedded values affect dialogue. The sociocultural background from which Freire's theory emerged, the oppression of the masses in Brazil by an elite who reflected the dominant values of a non-Brazilian culture, resulted in him depicting the objectified culture as being false and hostile to the culture of the indigenous learner. The crux of Freire's argument is that no education can be neutral since the culture of the oppressed is in opposition to that of the elite. Freire (1974) adopted the term 'conscientisation' to describe the process whereby people come to understand that their view of the world and their place in it is shaped by social and historical forces that work against their own interests. He argues that the oppressed lack a critical understanding of their reality, thus the emphasis in learning from a Freirian perspective is on the dialogue between the teacher-learner and the learner-teacher. Freire regards the teacher as a facilitator who is able to stimulate the learning process (rather than one who teaches 'correct' knowledge and values).

However, although Freire dealt with issues of power and oppression, much of his work is largely disregarded, or unknown in most disciplines in higher education. This is perhaps reflected through the fact that universities are increasingly *not* spaces of interrogation, refutation and equality of speech and acts, particularly with the increasing erosion of academic freedom. Discussions with colleagues often shift beyond debate into the edges of conflict, which perhaps could be the beginning of creating and reclaiming spaces of interrogation.

Dialogic conflict

A space in which dialogic conflict occurs is not only difficult to manage in terms of the escalation of conflict within a conversation, but also in the spaces beyond the initial discussion where the conflict emerged. However,

Gadotti (1996: xi) has argued that conflict has a productive place in dia-logue, since he suggests 'there is no kind of peaceful transformation'. Most dialogic conflict begins as a difficulty, as a small fracture, rather than a high-level dispute. Yet often in issues of transformation, such as that raised by Gadotti, where prejudice, habits and diverse behaviour are under debate, the conflict may escalate in the following three major phases.

Phase One emerges when an enlargement of the dialogic conflict occurs, as the parties focus on emphasizing the differences that exist between them. Whatever the focus of the difference, the fracture comes under stress from the increasing demands of the parties and so the community begins to experience disintegration – a breaking of its unity – and division. During this phase the emphasis is always on what we are that they are not, and what they are that we are not. Three shifts take place in the relationship. First, the parties move from focusing on what they have in common to focusing on the differences between them. This in turn leads to physical distancing between them – they spend less time together and they avoid one another whenever they can. Finally, the parties begin to attribute destructive behaviours to each other and begin to see the others as constituting a danger. This final shift in Phase One results in a compounding of the break in the dialogic conflict.

Phase Two is characterized by the parties losing sight of their own faults and increasingly ignoring any common ground or similarity with 'the enemy', and both sides begin to move apart. There are three main concerns for the parties during this second phase. Both sides seek to deal with their inner stresses through a process of identity building. They seek strength and conviction for their cause and so attempt to develop:

1. A united front
2. External support and a good public image
3. A position of strength from which to strike against the opposition.

Phase Three sees the emergence of power dynamics and power-ridden dia-logue, as one or both parties assess the gap to be so wide that they then think they have the right, the will and the ability to destroy the opposition without too much collateral damage. Phase Three sees the parties locked into open confrontation and the longer the conflict continues, the more desensitized the parties become. The consequences of Phase Three may result in a per-manent split of the parties and the break-up may result in one or neither surviving, or in a permanent breakdown of all parts.

Although authors such as Rogers (1983) have argued for unconditional positive regard in our relationships and conversations with others, and Habermas suggests reciprocity, there is relatively little in the academic canon that helps or guides us in seeing how such complex and difficult discussions about equality and reciprocity can be learning spaces. When ideas or theories are discussed and argued about and different perspectives emerge between colleagues in most universities, worldwide, there is a sense that such debate is a sign of a healthy academic community. However, there are occasions when the discussion is perceived to be a personal attack, or actually is a personal attack and the discussion escalates into a conflict. For example, in the process of undertaking some informal peer assessment for a colleague, I asked him to explore his pedagogical stance; the choices and decisions he made as a teacher. After some discussion I suggested that perhaps a less authoritarian approach may be more appropriate towards students at Master's level. Part of the difficulty was that having never seen my colleague teach before, but having spent considerable time with him in debate, I had assumed he would use a more discursive rather than authoritarian approach. My colleague's response to my suggestions was one of anger and confusion, and clearly a sense of disjunction which resulted in him refusing to discuss his approach. The questions I had asked were too challenging and had resulted in dialogic conflict. This prompted me to realize how little we discuss our positions as teachers, the ways in which we use power in learning situations and, perhaps more importantly, how we view and manage conflict and disjunction in dialogic spaces. This illustrates the difficulty of 'heteroglossia' (Bakhtin, 1981); the coexistence of distinct varieties within a single linguistic code whereby there is interplay of meanings and understandings, since the nature of heteroglossia arises from its social use by individuals and by communities.

To discuss our stances and our views on power and control can be difficult and troublesome for many of us, but to do so creates important sites of learning about our selves, as both learners and teachers. In short, as teachers, we seem not to use enunciative spaces (Spivak, 1988) in which we are able to speak both about what it means to be a teacher and to have a sense of agency in terms of questioning the political and pedagogical context of our work. To engage with such enunciative spaces could be seen as 'creative destruction' (Schumpeter, 1934) in an organization, whereby particular innovation challenges and destroys established practice. By creating opportunities to displace some traditional practices, or to critique practice in the light of new ones, is to create spaces for new ways of being and operating, that stretch beyond the hegemonic and authoritarian practices that continue to abound in higher education.

Language in dialogic spaces

What is often forgotten in dialogic spaces is that language is drawn from contexts and embedded meanings in texts, what Boughey (2006: 2) refers to as the 'received tradition'. Boughey (2006) questions the extent to which engagement is an autonomous skill, since the rules of engagement are formulated by academic expectations and traditions which students need to learn in order to participate in academic dialogues, processes and practices. Thus the way in which staff present a text to students locates their position in terms of the values and purpose they accord to it. Boughey (2006) argues that the notion of skills is problematic and suggests that texts may be seen by students, in terms of their tenor as:

- Didactic texts – students assume that texts inform them as to how things *should* be
- Producing texts – students believe their work should reproduce regarded texts and thus feel discouraged when they are criticized for reproducing facts
- Distinguishing voices – the idea that an academic text comprises multiple voices, those voices used by the author to substantiate their position as well as the solo voice of the author. While academics are able to recognize and locate different voices, students are not always able to distinguish voices and see books and articles often as flat textual pieces
- Taking a position – students do not often understand that taking a position means adopting a stance that is substantiated by others and not about personal experience. She argued (Boughey 2006: 10–11) 'To be right you have to draw on the right context in the right way'.

Thus language skills in dialogic spaces are deeply related to issues of identity, both for students and academics, and are not asocial, acultural or apolitical skills.

Entitled to speak?

Cockburn has suggested through her work on the exploration of under-standings of national identities that: 'Dominant groups maintain hegemony for the most part by discursive means rather than direct force, mobilising consent by inclining us toward particular identifications' (Cockburn, 1998: 213). University systems define and control us through both discursive and linguistic devices (for example what is discussed and what is not, the kind of language that is acceptable and not acceptable) and through risk mini-mization. Protocols about who is allowed to attend which meeting to discuss particular aspects of academic life limit dialogic space production, as well as limiting the way in which information is communicated. Although many universities use systems of sharing managerial information from the senior executive such as roadshows and monthly briefing documents, there is little real opportunity for dialogue to occur. When the executive team turn up to share their latest findings on the staff satisfaction survey, it is a brave lecturer who tries to create a dialogic space. Thus staff are inclined to assent, or acqui-esce, through apathy. Too many discussions are controlled and managed, and controversy is suppressed rather courted.

Yet dialogic control can also be seen in the way in which staff are consigned to formal categories through which rights and responsibilities are assigned, and corresponding behaviours are expected. Such delineation of identity is not only a form of dialogic control. It is also a means of ensuring staff recog-nize that they are expected to feel part of a community or at least come to an understanding about its rules, and how those who have become favoured reacted to their promotion to a higher position within that community.

The concept of dialogic spaces not only relates to the positioning of dialogue between staff and between staff and students, but also to a wider political debate. Although there has always between discontent in academe, the worldwide educational reforms of the 1990s have resulted in a new ruthlessness and a number of overbearing ideologies. For example, productivity, lifelong learning, enterprise and individualism are a few of the ideologies that are rarely discussed or examined, yet their overbearing presence has had an impact on learning spaces in a detrimental way. The new ruthlessness and its ideologies have brought with them a new language of higher education which is not unproblematic and has at its heart not only the control of higher education, and the higher education sector, but also dialogic control.

There is a sense that we choose not to speak into political spaces, because to do so might take up time which would prevent productivity. Thus as academics we may mimic a political position but in reality we largely choose to avoid political dialogic spaces. To speak against the new ruthlessness, new policies and new language of higher education is likely to be seen as disruptive and is likely to cause difficulties for the speaker. To speak against enterprise and to stand against the selling of academic souls to the productivity devil is a risky business. Perhaps then sabotage is our only option. Yet how might dialogic spaces be recaptured? The work of Smyth et al. (1997) on the creation of enunciative space is helpful here. The enunciative space (following Spivak, 1988) is defined as 'the opportunity to articulate what it means to be a teacher, to tangle with social issues beyond the technicalities of teaching; and having some agency within which to question and challenge the wider structures surrounding teaching and learning' (Smyth et al., 1997). What is suggested by these authors from their research would essentially seem to be ways of professional place-making, which I suggest could be embraced by the higher education sector, in short:

- Creating the dialogic space so that conversations can occur and are not left to chance
- Undertaking confirmation and interrogation whereby confirmation is taking an appreciative stance towards something in order to both understand it and act upon it; whereas interrogation requires taking up a critical stance towards the work in order to problematize it
- Framing action so that it is possible to make practical decisions about future endeavours that are based around empirical, hermeneutic and critical questions.

However, the concepts of dialogic learning, dialogic reading and story-telling are also useful means of developing a sense of an entitlement to speak about political concerns and new forms of ruthlessness that continue to arrive at the door of academe.

Conclusion

Dialogic spaces are those that increasingly seem to be marginalized and ignored across the higher education sector. Although online dialogue seems to be increasing, the relative monologism of blogs (weblogs) and the free authoring that occurs in wikis tends not to create new or re-create old dialogic spaces. However, this linearity seen in wikis and blogs seems to be interrupted in discussion fora where it would seem that new dialogic spaces are emerging through online discussions. Dialogic spaces need to be framed, delved into, argued for and prized. To speak, to be entitled to speak and to share our perspectives is a vital space in academic life, and must be reclaimed so we are neither rendered, nor render ourselves, voiceless.

5

Reflective Spaces

This chapter explores the notion of reflective spaces, spaces that are often given much currency in the professional education of students but perhaps not used a great deal by staff. This chapter scrutinizes the literature on reflection which to date remains largely anecdotal and under-researched. It suggests that reflective spaces have many characteristics but that the most challenging and uncertain form of reflective spaces have a liminal quality. The later section of the chapter argues that it is only by engaging with cognitive mapping, complexity theory and risk that staff can begin to use reflective spaces that will interrupt the performative practice currently prevalent in academic life.

Reflection and reflective practice

One of the central difficulties about the concept of reflection in higher education is that so much has been written about it. Much of the literature discusses ways of enabling and developing reflection in students, yet relatively little has been considered about how to use reflection, reflective practice and, in particular, reflective spaces for staff. Further, the result of the magnitude and range of research and writing in this area has resulted in confusion about the terms and the ideas inherent within reflection and, perhaps more importantly, the ideas associated with it. The consequences are then that theories and ideas that relate to questions about reflection have diverse destinations because of their diffuse origins. For example, the literature related to reflection, reflective practice, the reflective practitioner and reflection in, and on, action informs the notion of reflective spaces but does not delineate such spaces.

Reflection is predominantly spoken about in terms of a sense making process and tends to be seen as:

- Thinking about experiences and ideas so as to discover new connections or conclusions to guide future action

- Self-appraisal of what we are currently doing to try to get a new or different perspective
- Evaluating and critiquing action – ours or someone else's action
- Searching our understanding to bring meaning to the surface
- There is also a sense of searching and self-discovery in some forms of reflection, for example, Gibran (1994: 67) suggests 'No man [*sic*] can reveal to you aught but that which already lies half asleep in the dawning of your knowledge'.

While there are many types and delineations of reflection the concept perhaps most useful to the idea of learning spaces is 'reflection in action'. This, according to Schön (1983), is a form of conversation with a situation that is stimulated by complex problems not easily solved by trial and error. Thus in the course of reflecting on a situation we are holding a conversation between the task and our own mental understanding of that task. Yet debates abound about what constitutes reflection, how it is used and the ways in which it develops and emerges in different people at different times. For example, Boud et al. (1985) stated that the capacity to reflect is developed to different levels in different people. Thus for some people reflection is just thinking about an issue, which is often characterized by a surface approach to reflection. Others may believe that structured reflection is vital for in-depth personal understanding. Boud et al. (1993) have suggested that it is possible to target reflection in three directions:

- Reflecting in advance is termed *prospective* reflection, it is what is designed and planned
- Reflecting immediately is termed *spective* reflection
- Reflecting on past events is termed *retrospective* reflection and can include a consideration of what could have been different.

However, other authors suggest that the idea of reflection is part of an emancipatory process through which we come to understand with more clarity both ourselves and our world. Much of this literature relates to the concept of learning spaces, since learning spaces are liminal in nature. The state of liminality tends to be characterized by a stripping away of old identities and an oscillation between states, it is a betwixt and between state and there is a sense of being in a period of transition, often on the way to a new or different space. Mezirow (1981) suggested that learning occurs as a result of reflecting upon experience. Thus content reflection is an examination of the content or description of a problem, process reflection involves checking on problem-solving strategies that are being used, and premise reflection leads the learner to a transformation of meaning perspectives (Mezirow, 1991). While these types of reflection encourage learners to think reflectively around their situation, in earlier work (Mezirow, 1981: 12–3) seven levels of reflection were suggested, of which some are more likely to occur in adulthood. These can be summarized as follows:

1. *Basic reflection* is an awareness of a specific perception, meaning or behaviour.
2. *Affective reflection* is an awareness of our feelings in relation to the specific perception, meaning or behaviour.
3. *Discriminant reflection* seeks to assess the validity of our awareness, such as is what I am seeing and feeling accurate?
4. *Judgemental reflection* is an awareness of the value judgements being made.
5. *Conceptual reflection* is an assessment of how adequate the concepts are that are being used to make an accurate judgement.
6. *Psychic reflection* is reflection on the way you normally make judgements.
7. *Theoretical reflection* is an awareness of the strengths and weaknesses of your approach to your perceptions.

As mentioned in Chapter 4, Mezirow argued that everyone has constructions of reality that are dependent upon reinforcement from various sources in the sociocultural world. Reflection is vital to ensure that our perspectives are transformed, and is part of an emancipatory process of becoming critically aware of how and why social and cultural assumptions have constrained the way we see ourselves. Mezirow described such emancipatory learning as that which involves an interest in self-knowledge and in gaining personal insights through critical self-awareness.

It is possible to align reflective spaces, in some ways, to levels of reflection. For example, in some reflective spaces we tend to go lightly over old ground – we reflect on problems, we share difficulties over coffee or during a walk. Yet there are other reflective spaces which are not just used for managing difficulties but are spaces where we penetrate actions and reactions, we drill down to examine layers of meaning and consciousness in an attempt to make sense of both problems and processes. Then there are further levels which concern the beginning of reflection of our meaning-making, our sense of life world and our sense of becoming conscious of the class, gender, race and stereotypical rituals that blind us to other possibilities. Thus reflective spaces are more complex than forms of, and ways of doing, reflection. Further reflective spaces are not merely bland therapeutic spaces into which one waits for inspirations to fall, and are often difficult spaces to inhabit.

Reflective spaces

Reflection, as discussed above, is seen in a number of ways. However, the formulations of reflective spaces referred to here are akin to those defined by Mezirow. Mezirow argued that reflection occurs in diverse ways, but it is higher levels of reflection that are important here. Thus it is at the points at which our constructions of reality are no longer reinforced by the forces of our sociocultural world that we begin to move from a state or position of reflection into reflective spaces. Thus although reflective spaces are not necessarily liminal spaces, they do have liminal qualities about them. The liminal qualities of reflective spaces generally seem to emerge at the points where there are moves away from reflection towards reflexivity. This is because reflective spaces are interstitial spaces, spaces at the margins, zones of revelation and movements towards understanding. To be in a position of transformational reflective space is reflexive, because it prompts an examination of beliefs, values and identity. One of the difficulties with the conception of reflexivity is that how you see it depends upon where you are coming from. As a concept it is deeply embedded in both our perceptions of self and our perspectives of the world, which ultimately are connected to our personal stance. Thus, when we are engaging with reflective spaces there is sense that we are located in an interrupted world.

Reflection as interruption

Reflection can be seen as interruption because reflection tends to disturb our position, perspectives and views of the world. Reflective spaces are locations of interruption because they are somewhat set apart from familiar work settings. Although such spaces may occur 'in' the familiar, such as the home or office, being in such spaces is less familiar or 'un'familiar. For example, to choose to spend time reflecting on an incident or a meeting while walking between buildings, or to write reflective accounts of a troublesome debate with a colleague may not be particularly unusual, but the process of engaging in such activities is tending to decrease with the busyness of university life. Yet to spend such time in these kinds of reflective space can render the familiar strange and thus open up opportunities for different forms of interpretation to occur. What I mean here is that creating places and opportunities for reflection not only enables the familiar to become less so, but also prompts us to reconsider issues and perspectives in new ways. The result is that our stances and perspectives are something that we continually meddle with through reflective processes that we have chosen to engage with consciously and regularly in everyday life. Thus we choose to interrupt everyday actions through reflections and interrupt current stances by attempting to expose new perspectives and positions.

Reflective spaces are therefore defined here as spaces that are pre-liminal or supra-liminal, they are invariably suspended states, metastates in which understandings emerge from often complex situations during the course of everyday life. These spaces seem to occur in the context of other activities and do not tend to result in an overarching stuckness, it is as if one is just stuck, or 'in liminality' in one particular area of one's life. Thus reflective spaces tend to sit at the borders of psychic and theoretical reflection, and to some extent affective reflection, and reflexivity.

Locating reflective spaces

One of the central difficulties of the idea of locating reflective spaces is that it is easy to assume that they are merely trite moments of metacognition; just created spaces to think about one's thinking. Similarly it would also be possible to see them as dialogic spaces, particularly soliloquizing dialogic spaces, such as that undertaken by Hamlet and discussed in Chapter 4. Yet reflective spaces differ from dialogic spaces because the processes involved are not concerned with interaction and conversation, but instead are related to shifts in one's personal stance. As mentioned in Chapter 1, personal stance refers to a particular position one takes up in life towards something, at a particular point in time. Stance is not just a matter of attitude; it encompasses our unconscious beliefs and prejudices, our prior learning experiences, our perceptions of tutors, peers and learning situations, and our past, present and future identities. It is our stances that are on the move in reflective spaces, although, as will be seen later, the extent to which it is about our stance or our identities that are shifting depends very much upon the kind of reflective space we find ourselves in. However, in the process of reflection, of whatever sort, we tend to move into a metastate which results in shifts in consciousness that occur at three levels:

- Primary: where rudimentary levels of reflection occur, such as thinking about experiences
- Transitional: where a challenge or query has promoted reconsideration of one's views and perspectives
- Transformational: where a major challenge to one's position and identity has occurred, often resulting in a sense of confusion and a need to radically rethink one's stance.

While these levels are presented as three different spaces, they are interconnected and overlap. Nevertheless, it is more likely that transformational reflective spaces have a liminal quality than primary spaces, because catalysts to change and major epiphanies tend to prompt identity shifts.

Primary reflective spaces

Primary reflective spaces are where rudimentary levels of reflection occur, such as thinking about experiences, and exploring ideas and challenges. Many of us encounter these spaces daily and in many ways these are seen as rudimentary levels of reflection, which invariably do not reach beyond validity testing and problem-solving strategy problems. They include problem-solving and a prospective challenge.

Problem-solving
Although there is considerable literature on problem-solving and types of problems, the forms of problems that are encountered in primary reflective

spaces tend to be everyday challenges that require us to understand the difficulty and attempt to respond to it. Such problems tend not to be messy problems but instead are those that challenge us to seek explanations. Furthermore, they tend to demand the use of either *spective* reflection (immediate reflection) or *retrospective* reflection (reflecting on past events). Yet the questions we ask ourselves can guide the ways in which we engage with the issues. Thus, in the case of reflective spaces, to reconsider a conflict and ask ourselves, 'What is the matter with this man?' results in our seeking explanatory knowledge, knowledge that offers some reason for the difficulties we are experiencing rather than 'What is the matter with me?' This is a moral dilemma problem that is likely to result in engagement with transitional reflective spaces.

A prospective challenge
A different form of primary reflective space is encountered when considering a challenge. This prospective reflection helps us to consider difficulties in advance and how it may be possible to deal with them. However, prospective reflection can also be seen as anticipation, either of a challenge or as something one would wish for but may not have. For example, in the poem 'Roman de la Rose' de Lorris (1270–7) describes a rose in a walled garden, the interior of which represents romance, with the exterior being everyday life. The rose is seen as a symbol of love but it is seen to be just out of reach, symbolizing unattainability. Thus the pleasure and the anticipation is in seeking to gain what might be out of reach.

Reflections at a primary level do not *generally* prompt us towards engagement with disjunction. Consider our own position within the conflict. More active dimensions of reflection tend to force a shift away from primary reflection which focuses on validity testing, and prompt us to consider our own position in relation to others, thus moving us towards a reinterpretation of the situation and not just a reflection upon it. Although initially it might seem that reflective spaces are those which we choose to be in, they are often spaces in which we find ourselves – sometimes unexpectedly. For example, when beginning to write or to plan a speech it often helps to site ourselves in a reflective space in order to consider what it is that we want to say. Yet when struggling with an idea or attempting to find a way of portraying a concept, we often move into a transitional reflective space; thus the notion of challenge is central to the idea of transitional reflective spaces.

Transitional reflective spaces

Transitional spaces are encountered when a challenge or query prompts us to reconsider views and perspectives. Transitional spaces have a sense of movement from one position to another. Therefore, shifts in position occur in particular areas of peoples' lives, at different times and in distinct ways. The notion of transitions carries with it the idea of movement from one place to another, and with it the necessity of taking up a new position in a different place. Leaving your existing position and entering the transitions can be fraught with difficulties that may result in further transition. Thus transitions can often be difficult and disturbing, and yet simultaneously be areas where personal change takes place. However, there would seem to be two particular forms of transitional reflective space, those that are disjunctional and those that are liminal.

Disjunctional reflective spaces

Transitional spaces are spaces that largely appear to be prompted by enabling disjunction, whereby a difficulty or barrier is encountered that can then be managed in a dynamic way. Many staff have described disjunction as being a little like hitting a brick wall in learning and they have used various strategies to try to deal with it. It has similarities with troublesome knowledge (Perkins, 1999) in that it often feels alien and counter-intuitive. This is because it invariably feels a negative place to be, rather than a space for growth and development. Enabling disjunction is a space where staff realize and engage with a need to move away from their current position. Being in such transitional spaces is often prompted by a catalyst that might at first seem complex and irresolvable, since it requires a move from one life space to another. Life spaces are defined here as how one positions oneself in a particular context and the types of emphases one puts on different spatial zones one inhabits. For example, women who are academics and have young children may put more (or less) value on home life space compared with academic space. Thus they choose to position their life space values more within the role of a parent than an academic. Later in life the prospect of job promotion may prompt a transition towards a life space that focuses more on being an academic. However, the shift into a different life space is likely to be prompted by some kind of catalyst. These transitions are not normally transformational; rather they reflect a repositioning, a shift or a movement into a different life space.

Liminal reflective spaces (1)

Transitional reflective spaces, however, might also have a degree of liminality about them, particularly if they are spaces of surprise – spaces where one finds oneself unexpectedly. For example, sudden promotion, a death in the family or the breakdown of a relationship may create an unexpected position in a life space that is essentially liminal; it is betwixt and between. These kinds of spaces ultimately tend to result in transformation. For example, promotion may be a transition into a life space that has been much sought after. Thus this space is transitional not transformational. However, in terms of liminality the sense of dis-ease that often occurs in liminal spaces emerges after the transition has taken place. For example, when a person is promoted and 'becomes' a dean, there is sense of being immediately 'positioned' into this new life space by others, but for that person the shift into being a dean may not be a straightforward transition, and it can often be difficult for the person to 'locate' themselves as dean. The notion of transition here relates to role shift; moving roles, rather than an identity shift, which is what occurs in transformative spaces. Role shift relates specifically to a change in one's role somewhere in the life space, whether this is promotion, change of employment or change in domestic role. Role shift is defined by the nature of a given (and often bounded) role, and change is associated with change in one's role; the set of connected, expected behaviours, rights and obligations as conceptualized by actors in a social situation; rather than in one's identity.

However, in the process of role shift, role confusion can occur, which is where, in a given situation, an individual has trouble determining which role should be played. There appears to be little recognition in academic life of this emotional suspension; the sense on the one hand that the individual has become someone else and moved into a new life space, while on the other hand their emotional intelligence, and their ability to perceive and engage with their own emotions and those of others, have not yet caught up and connected with being positioned in this new space. Further, as Ferreday and Hodgson have argued:

> This concept, *(of emotional intelligence)* originally suggested by Salovey and Mayer (1990) and popularised by Daniel Goleman (Goleman, 1995), focuses on the role played by emotion as a set of competencies that facilitate effective management and leadership, decision making and increasing productivity. At the same time, there has been increasing anxiety about the supposed 'emotionalization' of culture in the light of a growing 'therapeutic ethos', as Elaine Swan has noted (Swan, forth-coming). This is problematic in two ways: firstly because it understands emotion in an individualistic way through discourses of self improve-ment, and secondly in its suggestion that emotion is (or can be) a self-aware performance over which one has control. What is missing from this approach, we would argue, is both an articulation of the roles played by *specific* emotions in processes of knowledge exchange and construction and awareness of the performativity dimension of emotion. (Ferreday and Hodgson, 2007: 1, original emphases)

Reflective liminal spaces can be both troubling and affirming spaces, in the sense that they can be difficult spaces to inhabit, and the anticipation of locating oneself in such spaces can be disquieting. However, such disquietude can also be related to having made a choice, to choose is to make a decision about moving into a different place, and thus reflective spaces which become related to choice also bring with them a sense of responsibility about such choices. For example, choosing to apply for a professorship reflects our belief that we are ready for new status and responsibility, but to put ourselves for-ward for such a position is daunting and the new status and accountability that comes with it affects both professional and personal lives. The emotional adjustment to such a position is often a time of oscillation between states akin to the example Meyer and Land (2005) offer, regarding adolescence. Here adolescence is invariably a prolonged liminal state whereby behaviours similar to those of being an adult are mimicked. They argue:

Adolescence, for example, as an identified liminal state within modern Western cultures, often involves oscillation between states of childhood and adulthood. Adolescence may be a protracted liminal state and may involve behaviours which approximate to adulthood but constitute for a given period a form of *mimicry* of the new status. It would appear too that within liminal states the new status (eg adulthood, first-time mother-hood, manhood) is anticipated simultaneously both with desire and apprehension. (Meyer and Land, 2005: 376, original emphasis)

This notion of liminality and mimicry in adolescence can be seen in areas of higher education where a form of masquerade occurs in order to be seen to be relocated, when the individual concerned might not feel this to be the case. For example, the sense of 'becoming a professor' is a liminal state, whereby one has the title and responsibility but the emotional adjustment is such that mimicry occurs until the emotional curriculum vitae has caught up with the actual curriculum vitae. The sense of being in a complex liminal space such as this is rarely spoken of, and many staff only realize afterwards that being in such a liminal space results in initial struggles with the role, authority and requirements of the occupation. There remains some silence around the stories and struggles of becoming a professor, yet perhaps this is because those that have moved over the threshold have become part of the status quo that continues to support many of the hegemonic practices of academic life.

Transformational reflective spaces

While transitional spaces do involve some shifts towards 'becoming, moving and repositioning' into a different life space, transformational reflective spaces are more complex and involve an identity shift. This happens when challenges occur to value and belief systems. Identity shifts are characterized by not only a change in perception of self and others, but also changes in perspectives about the political, social and economic ways in which life is lived. These shifts are transformational because they are invariably caused by moral dilemma problems and result in perspective transformation. These spaces, then, are where a major challenge to one's position and identity has occurred, often resulting in a sense of confusion and a need to radically rethink one's stance. Much of what occurs in these spaces can be likened to the notion of a personal epiphany. A personal epiphany is an 'interactional moment' (Denzin, 1989: 70) which occurs when a challenge or set of chal-lenges results in a crisis or change to someone's meaning perspective. Epiphany is the Twelfth Night after Jesus Christ's birth, when he was visited by the Three Wise Men and his divinity was revealed to the world. It derives from a Greek word, *epiphainein*, meaning 'to manifest'. However, the main writer to extend the meaning of the word was James Joyce who was interested in sudden, dramatic and startling moments which seemed to have heightened significance and to be surrounded with a kind of magical aura. He referred to this particularly in *Ulysses* (Joyce, 1922).

The notion of epiphany has been developed in various ways, but in interpretative research Denzin (1989) has proposed four different types of epiphany that are useful in conceptualizing transformational reflective spaces:

- cumulative epiphany: an event that is symbolic of profound changes that may have been going on for a number of years, or be a turning point in one's life caused by the accumulation of numerous related experiences
- illuminative epiphany: a point in time or particular experience that reveals insights; or an event that raises issues that are problematic
- major epiphany: such as an event or experience that is so traumatic or challenging that its meanings or consequences are immediate
- relived epiphany: an event or issue that has to be relived in order to be understood.

Two examples are used here to illustrate transformational reflective spaces, since encounters with such spaces are specific to individuals and cannot be delineated by generalizable characteristics.

Liminal reflective spaces (2)
The state of liminality tends to be characterized by a stripping away of old identities, an oscillation between states and personal transformation. Liminal spaces are thus suspended states and serve as transformative in function, as someone moves from one state or position to another. The idea of a liminal state is taken from ethnographic studies into rituals, for example, rites of passage such as the initiation of adolescent boys into manhood. Turner (1969) adopted the term 'liminality' (from Latin *limen*, 'boundary or threshold') to characterize the transitional space/time within which the rites were conducted.

> These ethnographical examples relate primarily to liminality in life cycles . . . The concept of the 'betwixt and between' liminal state then becomes easy to recognise in contemporary western culture – think, for instance, of the wedding ceremony where the 'threshold' ceremony is followed by a 'liminal' honeymoon. Think, too, of funerary ceremonies where the period from death to inhumation (or cremation) is equally 'liminal'. (Trubshaw, 2003)

Liminal reflective spaces that also involve choice include writing spaces, particularly writing retreats, and some forms of digital spaces. However, reflective liminal spaces are constantly on the move and can either be temporary or more or less permanent. Transformational reflective spaces are not always, and not often, encountered through choice, and are often spaces in which one finds oneself to be located. For example, visiting an informal settlement in Cape Town challenged me to reconsider my understanding of poverty and privilege. While I had chosen to visit, I had not expected the disjunction and subsequent ongoing transformation that occurred. This was a major epiphany since the experience was traumatic, and one that not only resulted in new perceptions but a personal repositioning about the relationship between notions of privilege and being white, and yet I remain in a liminal space.

Transformational spaces then may not only be liminal, but may remain liminal. There is a sense in much of the literature (see, for example, chapters in Meyer and Land, 2006) that liminal spaces are those in which an individual stays for a time, and then emerges into a new place or position. Yet it would seem that the literature in higher education that addresses liminality has rather underplayed the complexity of it as a concept and as a position. Instead I would suggest that in some areas of our lives we tend to remain in liminal spaces for months, possibly years, before the dilemmas and concerns connected with the transformation are resolved. Furthermore, there is also a sense in which it is possible to remain in a liminal space alongside normal life, thus it is as if liminality is occurring at a metalevel where ideas and concepts are merging and at the same time, everyday living occurs on a parallel track.

It would seem that transformative reflective spaces might also be spaces in which the whole self is not necessarily involved, and that there is a dislocation so that identity shifts take place in a cognitive space alongside everyday life. However, much of the literature suggests that transformation and liminality occur in separate spaces from life – the idea that there is a removal from life in order to transform. Yet it seems that this is not always the case, and that transformative spaces can occur alongside life. This might be what staff and students often verbalize as feeling fragmented in new or challenging learning situations. When staff and students have spoken of a sense of fragmentation, my assumption was that such fragmentation was all encompassing, with their whole identity being in flux. Instead it would appear that only some areas feel fragmented while others do not. Perry (1970), in his study of Harvard students, argued that in the intellectual, ethical stages of development students reach position 6 whereby some areas of their lives felt in a continual state of disjunction and others did not. Thus transformative reflective spaces would seem to be characterized by fragmentation, the location of the transformation being in one or two areas (rather than the whole identity being in transition), and a strong sense of the shifts taking place but invariably at a metalevel, along with a sense of moving forward or some kind of resolution being within reach. The shifts are meta in the sense that they occur above and beyond everyday life; they are, as it were, suspended. Ultimately the shifts are likely to impact on everyday life and prompt changes in life spaces. However, it would seem that it is possible to stay in these meta-states over a period of time, until the disjunction has been resolved or the transition into a new life space has occurred. However, these can also be grouped into whether they are temporary or permanent as illustrated in Table 5.1.

Yet while it might be possible to locate issues as being more likely to prompt engagement with primary as opposed to transformational spaces, the level

Table 5.1 Forms of reflective spaces

Form of reflective space	Temporary	Permanent
Primary	Problem	
	Prospective challenge	
	Active reinterpretation	
	Retroactive reflection	
Transitional	Disjunction	Travellers
	Marginality	Priesthood
	Liminality (1)	
Transformational	Liminality (2)	
	Major epiphany	

and type of engagement relates to one's personal stance and identity. Thus reflective spaces are sites of difficulty as well as areas of pleasurable reflection and spaces where sense-making occurs. The location of reflective spaces for individuals will therefore relate to choices we make about how we place ourselves in relation to the issues about which we are reflecting.

Placing ourselves in relation to reflective spaces

The concept of placing ourselves introduces questions about the notion of space and place in academic life. Yet the notion of placing also relates to the notion of positioning. Space, as discussed in Chapters 1 and 2, is seen predominantly as a social product (Lefebvre, 1991), whereas place is more often seen as a 'locale,' as physical geography (Giddens, 1991), invariably characterized by presence. However, as is discussed in depth in Chapter 6, there are difficulties with these definitions since they become immediately problematic in online spaces where notions of presence change.

Online spaces cause some staff a sense of disembodiment, and therefore understanding of space and place collide, in ways that, at first glance, would seem to be unfamiliar in the world of face-to-face communication. At the same time there are issues about space and place in terms of how they are perceived and used in academic life. Thus reflective spaces are 'presumed' to be spaces rather than places; they are seen as internal cognitive spaces rather than as necessarily physical spaces which enhance opportunities for reflection, such as light rooms and silent spaces. For example, with the increasing 'noise' in higher education there is an interesting shift of academics to quiet cafés and restaurants. This cappuccino culture points towards the need to find alternative reflective spaces, spaces to think and plan. Phipps, for example, suggests that:

Thinking sounds like the soft turn of a page in a quiet, still library, where people go to think. Thinking also sounds like the animated, engaged hum of conversation with others who share common research interests. But this too is a nostalgic thought, for the quiet of libraries is now rarely a real quiet and most scholars flee from campus to go to other places to think, home, the quiet coach on the train, to archives, or to conferences where they can come together and think together, in the same way as they can in the coffee shops and bars that are off campus. The sounds of silence and the sounds of thinking conversations have slipped from the buildings that used to house them. With no common rooms how can there be common thought on campus? (Phipps, 2005: 9)

The need for thinking spaces, the sounds of 'thinking conversations'; Phipps's stance towards noise and sound suggests that reflective spaces are indeed moving off campus, because nowhere is there quiet space, there is too much noise everywhere.

Creating reflective spaces

While some of the options for creating reflective spaces would seem to be quite simplistic, such as making a conscious effort to use primary reflection as a means of reflecting on an incident while driving home or walking the dog, there are some important points to be made. Reflective spaces of whatever sort are marginalized in the academic canon. Yet the importance of reclaiming such spaces is vital in order to have a sense of our own place and position in academe. To be dislocated, voiceless and lacking in reflexivity as an academic community will increasingly result in problems of representation. Thus some strategies for re-engaging with reflective spaces might be to utilize cognitive mapping or embrace complexity theory.

Cognitive mapping

The notion of cognitive mapping, as represented by Jameson (1991), is concerned that in a society where 'the newer allegory is horizontal rather than vertical' (Jameson, 1991: 52) it is important that we come to understand coexisting and multiple worlds, and that we see and understand that others see our own world(s) as partial and situated differently. Jameson argues that a notion of cognitive mapping 'require(s) the co-ordination of existential data . . . with an unlived abstract conception of the geographic totality' (Jameson, 1991: 52). Thus for every map which is produced there is an infinite number of other maps, 'a coexistence not even of multiple and plural worlds so much as of unrelated fuzzy sets and semi-autonomous sub-systems whose overlap is perceptually maintained like hallucinogenic depth planes' (Jameson, 1991: 372). Jameson uses the idea of the decentred and fragmented postmodern subject, and suggests a method of representation using cognitive mapping. By using such systems of mapping and understanding reflective spaces, it will be possible to make choices about engaging with higher forms of reflective spaces. Thus this idea of cognitive mapping might provide the means by which academics can position themselves within the system and reconcile that position with the other 'maps,' and even other roles at work and home within which they coexist. However, mapping will not merely be a performative or functionalist practice. This is because, in both charting our own reflective spaces, and engaging in other spaces we encounter by surprise, we will gain an in-depth understanding of the way our academic identities engage with the maps, charts and geographies of the reflective spaces terrain. Yet, complexity theory could be seen to take cognitive mapping further or perhaps overlay it, through what might be termed an iterative web.

Complexity theory

Although complexity theory is not generally located within a specific body of literature it is a theory that 'challenges the nomothetic programme of universally applicable knowledge at its very heart – it assents that knowledge must be contextual' (Byrne, 2005: 97). Such theorizing is not to suggest that everything is complex and deeply troublesome, but instead that it may be used to locate and redefine notions of coherence, identity and complexity in ways that offer a wider view of reflection, reflexivity and the ways in which they are located in the geography of higher education. This form of theorizing can help us to see reflective spaces as an iterative web. In such a web issues of context, identity and cultural practice can be (re)considered and the interrelationships between them explored.

Reduce performativity and increasing risk

There is a sense that, in the unstable state of higher education, the continual renegotiations of frameworks, structures and ideals mean that we are, in a sense, always in crisis. Reflexive modernization, the process by which the classical industrial society has modernized itself, has resulted in a sense of crisis characterized by a 'risk society' (Beck, 1992). This type of society with its emerging themes of ecological safety, the danger of losing control over scientific and technological innovations, and the growth of a more flexible labour force, will have a profound effect upon higher education.

Ways of managing this fragmenting culture might be seen not just as living with risk but as living in the borders, not moving towards the end of higher education or the end of the university, but along the brink, along the edges of the end. Yet, whether it is in the redesign of the curriculum, or in a new mechanism for ensuring performance through appraisal systems, or in some other 'innovation', there is the new language of higher education, the constant mantra that can be heard across campus, whose subtext is about minimizing risk. Whether this is an attempt to rein-in postmodernism or whether it has more to do with problems of representation is not clear. However, reflective spaces, of whatever sort, can offer the opportunity for engaging with risk, reducing solid learning spaces and re-creating other spaces. To do this it is important to minimize performativity through continually questioning the imposition of performative practice and instead of adopting it, finding alternatives. Living life in reflective spaces is uncertain, but it is important that it does not become performative and risk free.

Conclusion

This chapter has explored conceptions of reflective spaces, suggesting the whole notion of reflection needs not only to be recovered, but also redefined for use in the academic community. Reflection is not a basic process that should just be used in the undergraduate curriculum to help students to consider their learning and to develop so-called deep approaches to learning. Instead, reflective spaces need to be seen as transformative positions from which change, reflexivity and new stances can emerge. Space for reflection needs to be recaptured through activities such as writing retreats, debates and conferences; spaces where dialogue rather than didacticism is central. Perhaps, more importantly, spaces need to be developed at conferences for reflection, where being alone, thinking and developing reflexive positions are valued and sharpened. Providing such opportunities in face-to-face contexts and offering silent solitary spaces will enable greater links and understandings to be made between reflective spaces and digital spaces.

6
Digital Spaces

Introduction

This chapter considers digital spaces and the way in which electronic communication is now creating more and different spaces for learning, discussion and knowledge creation than in former years. It begins by examining what might count as digital spaces and then suggesting that virtual spaces are becoming increasingly liquid with the advent of Web 2.0 technologies. The way in which electronic learning environments can be constricted spaces as a result of over-management of the learning space is also explored. The latter section of the chapter explores formulations and locations of digital identities, in particular notions of electracy, embodiment and mobile learning.

Locating digital spaces

The difficulty with the perception of digital spaces is that there is often a sense that they are seen as being dislocated from physical spaces, and yet they are not. Web spaces are largely viewed as necessarily freer locations where there is a sense that it is both possible and desirable to 'do things differently'. The consequence is that digital pedagogies tend to be, or at least feel, less ordered than much face-to-face learning, forcing a reconsideration of how learning spaces in digital contexts are to be constituted. Digital spaces demand that we confront the possibility of new types of visuality, literacy, pedagogy, representations of knowledge, communication and embodiment. Thus, as Pelletier has argued, 'technologies are systems of cultural transmission, creating new contexts within which existing social interests express themselves' (Pelletier, 2005: 12). Through digital spaces, opportunities have been created for staff to shift away from two-way communication provided through lecture theatres and books, and has prompted the use of more dialogic approaches to learning. Despite such opportunities, there are still many who argue that there has become a sense of ordinariness in digital spaces. For example, Herring (2004) has questioned whether anything is really 'new' in digital technology, arguing that text messaging languages are just different codes from those used by teenagers, who developed handwritten codes before texting existed, and that blogs are merely reflective diaries. Yet there still is a newness about digital spaces because of the sheer dependency most academics have on computers and Internet access for writing and communicating. Admittedly the telephone and television changed the way 'modern' life was lived, but for most academics the speed of the postmodern world and the all encompassingness of digital technology may not be 'new' but has changed ways of thinking and practising very rapidly.

Yet there seems to be relatively little understanding of how digital spaces are constituted, how they might be mapped, how they might be used differently, and the impact that such spaces are having on the nature of higher education. For example, the provision of information for students, the structuring of learning, the development of websites and learning materials, and the changing in patterns of communication are some of the noticeable but probably smaller impacts that digital spaces are having on the higher education experience for staff and students. Yet the lack of in-depth longitudinal studies in this area introduces questions about how enhancing, or damaging, digital technologies are on student learning. There remain conflicts about whether 'pedagogy must lead the technology', a stance Cousin (2005) believes has become something of a mantra. Yet although this position would seem plausible and convincing to adopt, it denies the difficulties inherent in putting technology in the lead. It seems that many of the difficulties about the relationship between pedagogy and technology stem from a failure to ask what might appear to be some straightforward questions, such as:

- What do we mean by pedagogy in online spaces?
- For what is the *learning* technology to be used?
- Is it *learning* technology, *teaching* technology, technology to enhance teaching and learning, or something else?
- What is the relationship between the type of pedagogy to be adopted and the type of pedagogy currently being used?

Cousin (2005) also points out that technology is not just lying there waiting for pedagogues to put it to good use – but it might be that that is how some innovators see the situation. Yet it is important to understand what is meant by digital spaces.

Digital spaces are defined here as those spaces in which communication and interaction are assisted, created or enhanced by digital media. Most often in the recent past, digital spaces have been seen as those necessarily connected with the Internet. However, with the digitization of television and radio, digital spaces are now seen in a wider sphere than just the opportunity to enable learning with and through the Internet. Thus, digital spaces are not just virtual spaces, but are spaces affected and created by diverse media that impact on academic lives and influence the ways in which staff and students view and review the world. For example, interactive television and radio formats expect audiences to vote, telephone and engage with the Internet while watching and listening. Activities such as serious games are having an impact on the kinds of expectations students have about the use, expectation and necessity of digital media. Furthermore, podcasting and enhanced podcasting are increasingly changing the way students interact with learning materials, lecturers and their peers. Research into the impact of these media, and mobile learning, in particular, is still in its infancy, but what does appear to be apparent is that they are popular with students who download them regularly, although the extent to which the casts are used is not yet clear.

Deconstructing digital spaces

Digital spaces have changed, and continue to change, both the nature of higher education and the way in which learning is enacted within it. While digital spaces have brought new freedoms in terms of the ability to coauthor texts across the Atlantic, engage in e-conferencing, (re-)create identities through avatars and games, and provide access to a diverse range of knowledges, such freedom is not unproblematic. For example, many of these freedoms also bring within them covert expectations such as fast response times to emails and new linguistic and communication rules. It is expected that there will be no flaming or lurking, emails will be short, and clear subject headings will be used in discussions. Further issues about email usage and engaging with discussion lists continually raise controversy in departments about whether such engagement is a requirement or a choice. Such expectations can even be seen in professorial job descriptions where 'competence in using email' has been listed in the person specification as a requirement for appointment.

Digital spaces have also resulted in discussions and concerns about both containments and exteriorization in online environments. Containment is particularly evident in virtual learning environments (VLEs) such as WebCT and Blackboard that structure and manage learning. While many learning technologists have argued that much of the difficulty for academics is that they do not know how to use VLEs in innovative ways, the difficulties for the academics is that they believe that the technology disables rather than enables the pedagogy. Thus, creativity is prevented through the quest for linearity and maintenance of control. Three particular illustrations exemplify containment:

1. The lack of creation and loss of social spaces in online learning, for example, social spaces are used by students, such as MySpace and Facebook, but such spaces are rarely used as learning spaces since their very synchronicity renders them problematic for lecturers. As Land has argued:

   > The Web, for example, remains unruly, risky and troublesome, an implacable aspect of the supercomplexity and intractability of the

post-modern condition. An intriguing irony is that though current commercial virtual learning environments (themselves global corporations) might be seen as spaces that displace older collegial spaces, symbolised by the quadrangle, they nonetheless still attempt to wall in their own 'onscreen real estate', to fend off, perhaps, the post-modern wildness of the Web. In this respect they function as an *ordering strategy* (Land and Bayne, 2006). Like many modernist practices and spaces, they are singularly rectangular. (Land, 2006: 108: original emphasis)

Although some students may use the web as a social space within designated learning discussions designed by staff, the notion of social discussion in learning forums are invariably seen as 'interruptions'. Such interruptions are often closed down by staff when they 'moderate' discussions, indicating what is allowed and disallowed within such a learning space and deciding what counts as being professional and what does not. Yet it is rare in face-to-face seminars to see such policing tactics in action and social discussion largely goes unnoticed or is seen as part of the learning in interactional group work. Thus it would seem that the perceived unruliness of web-based discussions result in staff wanting to control and contain discussions in ways they might not have done formerly.

2. The 'required' labelling of subject headings in discussion fora in order that the discussion threads can be managed tends to overorder online interaction. The rules and codes for appropriate interaction are understandable in terms of courtesy and respect, given the reduced social cues in online spaces, but regulation can displace creativity and dialogue in favour of an ordering strategy. While this example might seem insignificant, it is one that is troublesome for those wanting to manage digital environments and contain discussions – something that is not possible in face-to-face meetings. Such management is redolent of what Taylor is referring to whereby terms such as 'boundaries' and 'sites of enclosure' are used 'to describe attempts by institutions to create contexts – enclosed territories – in which only the occupants define the particular rules and practices which govern internal operations' (Taylor, 1999: 11).

3. A new language with a subtext of control is evident in many VLEs, not only through semiotics, symbols and terminology, but also in the way learning is ordered, in ways that suggest how teaching and learning should be. The fact that VLEs are fraught with images that are deeply problematic and which seem to offer scaffolding, structure and safety, suggest stability and control. Further, all these systems encourage students not only to manage knowledge but also to manage their discussions and possibly even to think and learn in linear ways. However, there are further difficulties with the language of online learning. The notion of 'moderating' clearly locates the control with the lecturers. The notion of 'lurking' implies that silence and watching are inherently bad, while at the same time raising questions about what counts as presence in digital spaces – and who decides.

This kind of ordering and containment seem to reflect a more modern than postmodern stance to learning in a digital age. Yet perhaps it is the risk and troublesomeness of the web that prompts staff to retreat into familiar forms of control. Thus, the way in which technology is employed in many universities is resulting in the sense of an institutional panoptican, where visibility and calculability are not seen as problematic. Such 'exteriorisation' (Land, 2006: 101) seems largely to be ignored by both staff and students. This would seem to some extent to be a reflection of modernity rather than postmodernity, or perhaps more accurately the VLE could be seen as a fundamental example of 'solid modernity'. Bauman (2000) suggests that in the age of solid modernity there was a sense that accidents, and sudden or surprising events, were seen as temporary irritants since it was still possible to achieve a fully rational perfect world. Thus, solid modernity was characterized by slow change, where structures were seen as being tough and unbreakable. Technology in many ways gives a sense of linearity, rationality and the possibility of perfection. Thus in the development of online learning the technology is not to blame since once there is enough knowledge and technical skills, perfection is possible. For learners, the academics are the ones that get in the way of perfection. Yet it would seem it is in the very realm of digital spaces that solid and liquid modernity collide. Bauman has argued that we have moved into liquid modernity, the state of living in constant change characterized by ambivalence and uncertainty. Liquid modernity is thus a chaotic continuation of modernity. However, the solidity of technology would seem to overlay this notion of liquidity. For example, while Bauman suggests that the state of perfection can never be reached, there is a sense that those who design and implement learning technology, particularly large commercial organizations, seem to ignore this. Perfection for them is seen not only in terms of change, improvement and coded binaryness, but in the controlling of the technology, the normalization of spaces and the assumption about what learning should be and should look like. It might be argued that the shifting from one technology project to another characterizes liquid modernity, but in fact this masks the solid perfection of expectation inherent in the twenty-first-century conception of technology. For example, if as Bauman suggests, living in liquid modernity requires that we embrace emancipation and personal responsibility, there is necessarily a clash between liquid learning and solid technology.

Virtual learning or liquid learning?

Virtual learning environments do not easily allow for liquidity in terms of changing structures and visuality – although this is increasingly possible in some VLEs, it is relatively rarely undertaken by lecturers, and for many the semiotic impact is something they are not attuned to. Further, to change the structure and the appearance, to remove what is 'normal', is usually disliked by both the designers of the VLE and the university management systems –

for to allow emancipation is to allow too much risk in a world where increasingly 'corporateness' is all. To live in the liquid modern we need to act under the conditions of uncertainty, risk and shifting trust – none of which is a characteristic generally equated with VLEs. Liquid learning, as mentioned in Chapter 2, on the other hand, is characterized by emancipation, reflexivity and flexibility. Yet there is a tendency to move to innovative forms of learning, which allow for emancipation and criticality to emerge, but over time they often become increasingly solid spaces as the need to maintain and control overtakes the original desire for liquidity. Reverting to solid learning stances may result from organizational, institutional, peer or student pressure; yet, it might also be because liquid learning is inherently risky and taxing. However, this is discussed further in Chapter 8 in the context of troublesome spaces where a model of liquid learning is presented. Yet there are also difficulties with notions of embodiment, and arguments by many authors that we are not bodily located in online spaces.

E-liquidity?

Since the emergence of the Web 2.0 movement in 2004 there has been considerable debate about what constitutes Web 2.0 and what does not. Yet it would seem that the growth of this movement is liquid in nature and is something that is constantly developing and emerging differently. O'Reilly (2005) has argued that it 'doesn't have a hard boundary, but rather a gravitational core'. Others suggest that it does not refer to one development, but rather a series of emergent technologies such as Google, flickr, del.icio.us, wikis and blogs. However, as Alexander argues, 'Ultimately, the label "Web 2.0" is far less important than the concepts, projects and practices included in its scope' (Alexander, 2006: 33). Nevertheless it would seem that we may be moving very quickly into Web 3.0 technologies, whereby the focus is on content. 'Generation C' is being used to capture the idea that we live in an age of content producers. There is also a further shift to include not just content but context. For example, Cook (2007) has argued for the notion of Generation CX to capture this, and Bruns (2007) has suggested that we are not in the realms of 'produsage', a core activity of Generation C (and also possibly CX) and characterized by:

- Community-based – produsage proceeds from the assumption that the community as a whole, if sufficiently large and varied, can contribute more than a closed team of producers, however qualified they may be.
- Fluid roles – produsers participate as is appropriate to their personal skills, interests, and knowledges; this changes as the produsage project proceeds.
- Unfinished artefacts – content artefacts in produsage projects are continually under development, and therefore always unfinished; their development follows evolutionary, iterative, palimpsestic paths.

- Common property, individual merit – contributors permit (non-commercial) community use, adaptation, and further development of their intellectual property, and are rewarded by the status capital they gain through this process (Bruns, 2007: 4).

Pedagogically these developments have created new kinds of digital spaces, and such pedagogical formulations as wikis and particularly del.icio.us enable staff and students not only to set up their own social and academic bookmarking but also to share bookmarks, find academics with similar interests and create new research collaborations.

Despite such innovations and new liquid spaces, one particularly interesting area that is having an impact on learning spaces is the institutional decision about whether to use propriety VLEs such as Blackboard, or whether to user open-source solutions. Open-source software is defined as software where the source code, although under copyright, allows users to change and improve software that can then be redistributed in its modified form. The point of this is that it enables the product to be developed and those using it are seen as codevelopers. What is particularly interesting is the controversy this has raised. For example, the arguments by Lee (n.d.) at Oxford University suggest that using something like Bodington, an open-source VLE, is hugely desirable and probably costs as much as the time spent implementing Blackboard or WebCT. While institutional perspectives vary considerably, there remain questions to be asked about the pedagogical implications of proprietary software and the way learning is organized through it, both linguistically and semiotically. Further, the considerable costs of the licence fees for such VLEs are something that many universities still seem not to have unpacked sufficiently because of the argument offered that there is no provider support for open-source systems. For many academics, the somewhat clumsy and clunky VLEs available have encouraged many to opt for Moodle and Bodington, since they can be adapted more easily for institutional requirements and seem to be more flexible. For example, an academic was told recently by a learning technologist that the chat facility in WebCT had been turned off at the beginning of term because it was being overused, which would seem to indicate pedagogical shortsightedness. Examples such as this illustrate that technology can disable the learning and social integration of students, as well as student familiarization with new or different software.

However, one difficulty of the Web 2.0 movement seems to be some rather naive assumptions and impositions that appear to prevent engagement with complex issues from a critical perspective. For example, there are those (such as Bruns and Humphreys, 2005) who believe that current education systems are still text based and linear, arguing instead that wikis are not. Such views illustrate a naive stance towards wikis, which can be linear and may change relatively little over a year. Yet such perspectives illustrate that there are many in the digital community who lack in-depth understandings of models of knowledge and diverse approaches to teaching, learning and assessment. However, what is also of concern is the argument that in wikis and more specifically wikipedia it is possible, or even desirable, to have a neutral point of view. Knowledge sharing should surely provide opportunities for contestability and arguments rather than seek to manage them and close them down.

Digital identities

The idea of *having* a digital identity emerged predominantly from the notion of a mind–body split and the overarching sense when operating in cyberspace that there is a feeling of disembodiment and of not being present, a sense of being present and yet not being there. Such notions of (dis)embodiment appear to be troubling because they prompt us to consider the nature of our identities in cyberspace and whether they are the same or different from our other identities, and the ways in which we position ourselves in face-to-face encounters. Bayne (2005a) undertook research into staff and students' presentations of identity in cyberspace and found staff and students' experiences were reflected through two interrelated strands. These strands were, first, the difficulty staff and students experienced with the lack of visibility of the embodied self, which for some seemed to interrupt and prevent engagement in learning. Second, Bayne found that the technology often enabled a different but positive form of articulation of embodied selves. Bayne's work is clearly at the forefront of discussions about the pedagogical impact of digital technology on pedagogy. However, there seems to be little discussion in the e-learning and e-pedagogy literature about how and why it is that some people choose to portray themselves differently from their physical presence. The way in which we portray and project ourselves in digital spaces reflects how we see ourselves as learners and teachers. Thus, the complexity of being a learner and teacher in a variety of digital spaces introduces questions about what it means to 'be' a learner in these kinds of spaces, not only in terms of portrayal and presentation, but also in relation to pedagogy and action. For example, while there has been much discussion about presence and forms of presence in the literature on digital learning, there has been relatively little exploration of the impact of diverse forms of digital presence on pedagogy (see, for example, Feenberg, 1989; Bayne, 2005a; 2005b; Land, 2006). Moreover, pedagogy *in* digital spaces is continually changing and both this and the pedagogy *of* digital spaces are mutually shaping and changing each other. Thus issue needs to be considered in relation to:

- The effects of disembodiment on learning and communication
- Understandings of portfolios
- Managing gaps between literacy and electracy
- Mobile learning
- The impact of spatial organization on the construction of pedagogies.

The effect of disembodiment on learning and communication

Bayne (2005a) suggests that face-to-face encounters are still valued and preferred above online interactions. This would seem to be due to a number of factors, such as asynchronous speech promoting different kinds of interactions and language constructions rather than embodied speech. This is because by its nature asynchronous speech is unmediated both in terms of language and in relation to social cues. A further change is that in textual communication it is not always clear whether the author is present or not – often they are not, therefore the notion of what presence and embodiment mean in digital spaces is problematic. The way many staff 'cope' in this silent space is to (super)impose what they know in ways that fit with their cognitive perspectives and ontological understandings, largely because that is what they 'have'. Yet, those new to digital spaces tend neither to have a sense of how to be in, nor how to operate in, these spaces; thus there is often an overlaying of meaning to things that may go unnoticed in our other lives. For example, there are assumptions that lurking and flaming are necessarily disrespectful, when in face-to-face discussion not speaking or arguing would not necessarily raise concerns for others. The result is that our face-to-face stances impose pre-existing cognitive structures to online settings. What tends to introduce difficulties in digital spaces is not what we do not know, but what we do know; what we bring with us from our previous experiences which then we see no reason *not* to apply in the new setting. There is often an assumption that a 'digital space is distinctively different' but it might be that we are imposing difference on it because it is new and unfamiliar, which would seem to be a contestable position, just as is the notion that we are somehow disembodied in cyberspace. However, perhaps the question is really about whether or not the very fact that some people impose difference on it is enough to make digital space distinctively different? Thus, there is an assumption that because we are not 'seeing' non-verbal cues such as eye contact and body language, this is making online learning and communication difficult. However, it might be the case that new and diverse forms of communication are emerging that are creating new textual and identity formulations, neither previously located nor understood.

E-portfolios: the same and different?

One illustration of the way in which there is a tendency to impose temporal perspectives on learning in digital spaces is the e-portfolio. While there are clearly advantages in using the e-portfolio, such as ease of update, adaptability and presentation, it is not without disadvantages. Many authors see e-portfolios as an area of difficulty (Barrett and Carney, 2005; McAlpine, 2005; Tosh et al. 2005). Many professions have utilized portfolios for many decades, whether in art and design or health and social care. Tosh et al. (2005) suggest a number of concerns about the use of e-portfolios that emerged from their findings, such as:

- The need for buy-in by students
- Assessment practices
- Accessibility and technology
- Control over access
- Motivation.

While technology and access are significant concerns, buy-in, assessment and motivation remain problem areas in temporal portfolios. Yet other authors suggest that there are difficulties connected with presence and presentation. For example, McAlpine argued that:

> There is also a difference between the narrative identity embodied in the individuals as described by Ricoeur and the narrative identity embodied in the portfolio. In an individual the power to recast stories remains within the individual, who is free to reshape actions in the light of reflection, to construct new plots which over-power the old, and present them in a new temporal framework. However, in portfolios, the process of emplotment is laid bare through the reflective comments and feedback that is presented, as the power over temporal structuring is undermined by database structure, which affords equal value given to all entries. (McAlpine, 2005: 383)

Yet recasting stories, constructing plots and developing new plots occur in temporal portfolios. However, the extent to which one allows an e-portfolio database to order and privilege information and issues for one's self is a matter of choice, creativity, structure and selection of tool. A further difficulty that McAlpine suggests is that the use of an e-portfolio prompts the development of a virtual identity – yet it is not clear how or whether this is different (or the same) as the identities that are presented in a discussion board and in blogs. By contrast, Cohn and Hibbitts (2004) suggest that there is little evidence to support the e-portfolio as a pedagogical tool. What concerns the authors more though is the possibility that the growth in the use of portfolios will result in a tendency to use standardized prefabricated models. Such solid models will close down opportunities for creative e-portfolios, with a tendency towards summative objectives rather than seeing the e-portfolio as an emergent and formative artefact. A way forward suggested by Cohn and Hibbitts (2004) is a futuristic model termed a 'lifetime personal web space', which is:

> a beehive-configured Web space that possesses sufficient organizational plasticity to accommodate the user's developmental capacities and needs across a life time. The LPWS will thus be organized more like our brains than our file cabinets ... (it) would be structured according to the users' unique concept map ... not by predetermined institutional or commercial templates. (Cohn and Hibbitts, 2004: 1, 3)

Although the lifetime personal web space introduces questions about security, ownership, cost and the changes in technology to support it, both now and over its life span, it does raise interesting possibilities for linking together systems beyond those provided through wikis, blogs, MySpace and del.icio.us. Yet it might be argued that such spaces could be classed as electracy writ large.

Literacy and electracy

Ulmer suggests that just transferring and transforming literacy onto the Internet in the form of ready-made papers put on websites is not enough. Instead, he suggests that it is vital to create pedagogies that will enable the integration of Internet practices with literate skills in new and innovative ways. Thus, he suggests the concept of 'electracy', arguing that:

> what literacy is to the analytical mind, electracy is to the affective body: a prosthesis that enhances and augments a network of organic human potential . . . If literacy focussed in universally valid methodologies of knowledge (sciences), electracy focuses on the individual state of mind within which knowing takes place (arts). (Ulmer, 2003)

In practice, what Ulmer suggests is that electracy should provide learners with:

- Information that is customizable
- Opportunities to compose cognitive maps of their position within the field of collective knowledge (termed 'mystory', which comprises their story in the forms of a series of web pages of hypertextual compositions such as theorizing, images, symbols, links and personal narratives. The purpose of this activity is not only to learn how to create sites but also to record their learning and self-discovery through a biography)
- An opportunity to see writing as a selection of materials from archives
- Assessment that is not examination driven, but instead focuses on improvisation, thus students are given a question and asked to do something with it
- The ability to collaborate and be reflexive 'a promise and challenge of electrate education is to invent a pedagogy for group learning and self-knowledge' (Ulmer, 2003).

Much of what Ulmer is suggesting is the disruption of traditional ways of viewing learning and assessment, and interestingly he chooses to juxtapose science and arts. However, it could be argued that such disruption occurs in innovative forms of learning, that while still focused on literacy rather than electracy, do in fact offer opportunities for reflexive learning. Examples of such innovation would include action learning and problem-based learning, particularly where contestability and peer assessment is expected and accepted. In these kinds of learning the focus on the pedagogy is the assumption that everything is seen as contestable and the starting point in itself is not unproblematic. Further, with the emergence of new forms of problem-based learning online (PBLonline) it may be possible to suggest that a collision of literacy and electracy is a strong possibility, which will celebrate both forms rather than setting one against the other. Thus by utilizing a form of learning such as problem-based learning for critical contestability (Savin-Baden, 2000), students can be encouraged to make knowledge claims that are put before their team for examination by others in order to facilitate personal and pedagogical development. Individuals will thus be urged to use dialogue and argument as an organizing principle in life so that through dialogue they will challenge assumptions, make decisions and rethink goals. Thus by combining mystory with problem-based learning for critical contestability it should be possible to develop collaborative, contestable PBLonline that moves towards the possibility of a lifetime personal web space. While my own arguments as well as those of Ulmer may be seen as utopian, what is missing from both is the necessity of engaging with discipline-based pedagogy and the complexity of managing assessment. Ulmer, in particular, seems to largely ignore the latter. Apart from arguing for the marrying of problem-based learning with electracy, it could be argued that what Ulmer is suggesting also has many similarities with Winter et al.'s patchwork text (Winter et al., 1999). This is a means of students presenting their work in written form. Students build up text in course work over a number of weeks. Each component of work is shared with other students and they are expected to use different styles, for example a commentary on a lecture or a personal account or a book review. The focus in the patchwork text is on creation, recreation, reflexivity, collaboration and self-story.

Thus it would seem that some forms of problem-based learning, mystory and patchwork text are all 'forms' of electracy or literacy that attempt to reconstitute text and subject. However, what Ulmer's electracy proposes that the others do not is a clear setting out of the need to acknowledge and put into practice the notion that at the heart of learning is 'one's own being'. While the use of problem-based learning, patchwork text and action learning all locate the learner in a process, and acknowledge the importance of identity and identity shifts, these approaches are not as overt as mystory in terms of reflexive transformation.

Mobile learning

Mobile learning is defined as learning for learners on the move. Thus according to Sharples et al. (2005) mobile learning is based on the assumption that considerable learning takes place not only outside the classroom, but also that people create sites for learning within their surroundings. The MOBIlearn group defined the distinctiveness of mobile learning as:

- It is the learner that is mobile, rather than the technology.
- Learning is interwoven with other activities as part of everyday life.

- Learning can generate as well as satisfy goals.
- Control and management of learning can be distributed.
- Context is constructed by learners through interaction.
- Mobile learning can both complement and conflict with formal education.
- Mobile learning raises deep ethical issues of privacy and ownership.

One of the greatest foci on mobile learning in the early 2000s has been on podcasting and enhanced podcasting, whereby 'content' in its broadest sense is recorded in digital format and is then published via a website so that it can be downloaded onto a computer or mobile device. Although mobile learning, and in particular podcasting, is still developing and undergoing experimentation in higher education, there is relatively little research that has explored the pedagogy of mobile learning or examined how students use their podcasts. Mobile learning is a digital learning space that introduces challenges about what constitutes learning and pedagogy and, as the MOBIlearn group has noted, ethical issues are increasingly of concern. Further, as Sharples et al. conclude, with regard to mobile learning:

> We suggest that the implications of this re-conception of education are profound. It describes a cybernetic process of learning through continual exploration of the world and negotiation of meaning, mediated by technology. This can be seen as a challenge to formal schooling, to the autonomy of the classroom and to the curriculum as the means to impart the knowledge and skills needed for adulthood. Nevertheless, it can also be an opportunity to bridge the gulf between formal and experiential learning, opening new possibilities for personal fulfilment and lifelong learning. (Sharples et al., 2005)

The impact of spatial organization on the construction of pedagogies

Many authors (Jewitt, 2005; Bayne, 2005a; Land and Bayne, 2005) have argued that the imagery seen on screen is having an increasing influence over the way in which we manage knowledge, and make sense and meaning in higher education. The way in which digital spaces are created for staff, by commercial organizations that are politicized and contained by universities, and used by students enables, but perhaps more often occludes, ways of seeing where information is located. Bayne asks:

> If the spatial organisation and visuality of the screen both represents and *creates* a value system and an ontology, what social and pedagogical practices does the VLE interface reflect, inform and inscribe? What meaning does it produce? What version of pedagogy does it 'make visible' and what alternatives does it blind us to? (Bayne, 2005b: 2, original emphasis)

The lack of critical analysis of the impact of visuality on pedagogy is worrying. Further, there remains a conflict around what is allowed and disallowed in higher education, in terms of the control of knowledge and of the creation and maintenance of learning spaces. Digital spaces and particularly managed learning environments are areas that seem to provoke considerable conflict. For example, there appears to be a body of academics and learning technologists who argue that open-source components are vital, whereas others argue that there are sufficient tools within the VLEs to enable flexibility and collaboration. It would seem at first glance that it is those academics who prefer to control and patrol the borders of knowledge that also require the containment inherent in VLEs and the management of learning. Such academics dislike the disembodiedness and 'tech(no)body'-ness of wikis and blogs where knowledge and authorship is displaced and dislocated from the body of known forms and ways of being. Thus, there is sense that VLEs are the ultimate twenty-first century panopticon, where everything is visible, and for students or staff not to be seen in these spaces is a punishable offence.

Conclusion

Globally in most higher education institutions there is a requirement to use digital media for teaching, now resulting in most students using a virtual learning environment and probably fewer using textbooks than in the late 1990s. However, there still remains resistance by staff to use email and provide web resources for students. Digital spaces can prompt students to see knowledge not as something static and located in books, but rather something that is rich, varied, ongoing and contested. Knowledge to go, knowledge on the move is embodied by open-source systems and in particularly Web 2.0 technology. Yet what remains problematic is students' engagement with digital spaces: there seems to be a marked contrast between how such spaces are used by students within the university compared with what they do outside formal learning environments. For example, students may be seen on campus sitting outside the classroom, but off campus with an iPod in one ear, a phone in another and surfing the net at the same time. Yet there seems to be a reluctance to engage with VLEs and to use dialogue for learning in the same ways that they do extremely competently socially. Contained and restricted spaces will not be those in which creation and innovation occur. Thus if we are to embrace new and diverse formulations of digital spaces we need to embrace ideas such as electracy and open-source technologies, so that staff and students can become cocreators of digital spaces that facilitate new understandings of knowledge and foster the cultivation of diverse learning spaces.

Digital spaces are those that continue to be on the move; spaces that change with and through technology. The importance of such spaces in academic life is that they are changing learning in ways that as yet few of us understand. Yet pedagogy and digital change need to progress and inform one another together, not separately.

7

Troublesome Spaces

Introduction

This chapter explores the concept of troublesome spaces, spaces that prompt movement towards or into disjunction. However, a troublesome space might also be a space that seems dislocated from identity where the realization of being stuck is a sudden realization. Movement into such spaces may be caused by a number of catalysts, including issues such as prior learning experiences, threats to identity and threshold concepts. This chapter will begin by exploring the catalysts that generate movement towards disjunction. It will then focus on a model of transition that illustrates the relationship between catalysts to disjunction, student encounters with liminal spaces, and the possible options for dealing with disjunction.

Locating troublesome spaces

Troublesome spaces are places where 'stuckness' or 'disjunction' occurs. For both academics and students, becoming stuck in learning is often seen as deeply problematic rather than as being useful and transformative. Troublesome spaces are complex spaces since the process of becoming stuck and moving into a sense of confusion and fragmentation varies between people. The consequence is that an issue or situation that may become a troublesome space for one person may not do so for someone else. There are many catalysts that prompt movement into troublesome spaces that include:

- Modes of knowledge
- Perceptions of difficulty
- Disciplinary difficulty (including signature pedagogies)
- New learning difficulties
- Prior learning difficulties
- Threats to learner identity

- Threshold concepts
- Scaffolding learning
- Troublesome power
- Learning stances
- Challenging dominant narratives.

Modes of knowledge

Knowledge has been defined in a whole host of ways. Gibbons et al. (1994) have argued for Mode 1 and Mode 2 knowledge. Mode 1 knowledge is propositional knowledge that is produced within academe separate from its use, and the academy is considered the traditional environment for the generation of Mode 1 knowledge. Mode 2 knowledge is knowledge that transcends disciplines and is produced in, and validated through, the world of work. Knowing in this mode demands the integration of skills and abilities in order to act in a particular context. While this division has been popular and useful to many, it does to some extent reflect some of the problems of Ryle's (1949) notion of 'knowing that' and 'knowing how', which tends to both polarize and separate skills from knowledge. Although Mode 1 and Mode 2 knowledge are more complex and their position is better argued than that of Ryle, the problem with both of these stances is in the boundary spaces between the two forms of knowledge. Barnett (2004), however, argues for Mode 3 knowledge, whereby one recognizes that knowing is the position of realizing and producing epistemological gaps. Such knowing produces uncertainty because, 'No matter how creative and imaginative our knowledge designs it always eludes our epistemological attempts to capture it' (Barnett, 2004: 252).

What is missing from the arguments and formations of knowledge and knowing is not only the way in which the spaces between these forms of knowledge are managed, but also what it is that enables students and staff to make the connections between all of them. It might be suggested that the missing links here are disregarded forms of knowledge, for example, Cockburn (1998) suggests that knowing when to keep your mouth shut and the virtues of tact are forms of knowing that are required in many professions but are not forms of knowing that are made explicit in the academy. Disregarded forms of knowledge, then, might be termed Mode 4 knowledge since it transcends and overlays Modes 1, 2 and 3 knowledge, forming a bridge across the space between them. However, Mode 4 knowledge is also a mode in its own right, since it involves not only realizing and producing epistemological gaps, but also realizing the ways in which these gaps, like knowledge and knowing, also have hierarchical uncertainty. In contrast, Mode 5 knowledge is a position whereby one holds a number of modes together in a complex and dynamic way. Gaps, like knowledge, have hierarchical positions and this makes both the gaps and the knowledge, and the knowing and the knower eminently uncertain and liquid. The modes are set out in Table 7.1.

Table 7.1 Modes of Knowledge

Mode 1	Propositional knowledge that is produced within academe separate from its use and the academy is considered the traditional environment for the generation of this form of knowledge
Mode 2	Knowledge that transcends disciplines and is produced in, and validated through, the world of work
Mode 3	Knowing in and with uncertainty, a sense of recognizing epistemological gaps that increase uncertainty
Mode 4	Disregarded knowledge, spaces in which uncertainty and gaps are recognized along with the realization of the relative importance of gaps between different knowledge and different knowledge hierarchies
Mode 5	Holding diverse knowledges with uncertainties

The concept of disregarded knowledge encompasses knowledge often equated with emotional intelligence, such as when and how to use self-promotion, when to keep silent and when to intervene, but also with Haraway's (1991) concept of responsible knowledge – the need to take responsibility for the position from which we speak. Yet it would seem that this kind of knowledge is also akin to what Sibbett (2006: 137) refers to as nettlesome knowledge. Nettlesome knowledge comprises elements of knowledge that are taboo 'in that they are defended against, repressed or ignored, because if they were grasped they might "sting" and thus evoke a feared, intense, emotional and *embodied* response' (Sibbett, 2006: 137, original emphasis). Disregarded knowledge is neglected because it lacks status in academic life and is just that – disregarded. Furthermore, Taylor et al. (2002: 59) suggest that what is required is an expanded notion of knowledge and reason, so that the current narrow definitions of both of these concepts no longer dominate. For example, Midgley (1994) has remarked that epistemology has neglected a whole area of knowledge, that of knowing people. Also 'pressures to prepare students for employment often conflict with the desire to develop their critical faculties and to encourage them not only to participate in the production of knowledge, but to believe, too, that if they want to, they can change things' (Taylor et al., 2002: 66).

Haggis (2004) argues for learning that is social and relational, yet I would suggest that what she portrays using the voices of her participants is in fact disregarded knowledge, because it is about the idea of being able to function 'skilfully in a practical world'.

> People talk about giving, sharing, learning from each other, learning how to be sensitive to their children, and learning how to make things go smoothly in social situations. There is also a kind of learning that seems to be about *functioning skilfully in a practical world* . . . Others talk about problem-solving and common sense, verbal and relational skill (as opposed to a fear of writing), and make jokes about academics

who can't do basic practical tasks . . . people talk of finding out, reaching up, learning how to rise above tragedy, developing lateral thinking, taking away prejudice, getting answers, understanding, expanding the mind, and experiencing joy. (Haggis, 2004: 347, original emphasis)

The position here is essentially one of treasuring stuckness and sitting with chaos, it is a post-tacit and pre-realization phase and thus it has a liminal quality about it. It is a position of realization that emerges in a place of stuckness. It is a mode of knowledge, whereby one realizes that living with (and in) uncertainty is not a place to be reached or gained but instead is a place of transformation, a position of complex and dynamic chaos through which one learns to value stuckness in ways not previously understood. Further, Perkins's work is also useful here in understanding the impact of diverse forms of knowledge, and how this is often covert and therefore misunderstood by students, and often disregarded by staff (Perkins, 1999). More recently, Perkins (2006a; 2006b) described conceptually difficult knowledge as 'troublesome knowledge'. This is knowledge that appears, for example, counter-intuitive, alien (emanating from another culture or discourse) or incoherent (discrete aspects are unproblematic but there is no organizing principle).

Perceptions of difficulty

The difficulties with locating ideas of troublesomeness around 'knowledge', 'concepts' or 'theories of difficulty' seem to somewhat dislocate the concerns from the identities and biographies of learners and teachers. While the thresholds literature is both fascinating and helpful, apart from papers by Cousin (2006) and to some extent Land et al. (2005), there is a lack of ontological positioning in the studies. Thus there is a certain irony that they argue for mimicry being part of students not entirely engaging with a particularly threshold concept, and therefore not actually moving over the threshold. There is a form of mimicry occurring in the chapters by Davies (2006) and Meyer and Land (2006). For example, they argue that threshold concepts can be located, noticed and identified as generalizable concepts that can necessarily be embedded in a curriculum structure. Yet to argue for such a position immediately implies that threshold concepts are dislocated from learner identities. However, it is the overemphasis on the cognitive dimensions to threshold concepts, as delineated by Entwistle (2006), where this seems to be most apparent. For example, Entwistle argues that engaging with threshold concepts is related to *conceptual* change and relates his argument to Perry's conceptions of knowledge (Perry, 1970) and Saljo's conception of learning (Saljo, 1979). Thus, there would seem to be too much emphasis on conception and not enough on identity.

Disciplinary difficulty

To be able to communicate about differences at disciplinary borders it is important to understand both the notion of academic ethics and of academic citizenship. Until we have understood other disciplines within the faculty where we work, effective and transparent peer review systems and successful teaching innovation is unlikely to occur. Disciplinary differences are here to stay and can been seen not only in academic life, but also in the boundary spaces where work-based learning, academic disciplines, class cultures and perceptions of learning collide. However, there is hope. Dialogue is taking place in new spheres and diverse arena: at the boundaries of knowledge, at the borders of knowledge status and value and in new boundary spaces.

New learning difficulties

Many students who believe, on joining a course, that they understand what constitutes learning may not realize the challenges and conflicts that may ensue. For most, prior experiences will be of traditional, didactic methods of teaching that offered little opportunity for them to value their own knowledge and perspectives. However, students who then engage with active forms of learning, such as problem-based learning, are often challenged to explore and to develop their own tacit understandings and understand their incoherence. However, making sense of incoherence can be a precarious affair. Experience is not something that can be tied into neat packages, and thus to speak of it is to risk being seen as stupid and incoherent, when it is in fact the reflections upon those experiences which are incoherent. Meanings, particularly about prior experience and learning, seem to need eventually to become coherent in order that they can then be interpreted and subsequently valued.

Prior learning difficulties

Difficulties students have experienced in learning in the past, through didactic methods, then result in a belief that it is necessarily they who are unsatisfactory, rather than the course or the system. Thus many students' perceptions of themselves as failures or as individuals who find learning difficult are places where barriers to learning become evident. Other students often speak about the way in which their prior experiences of learning in didactic programmes have been both frustrating and isolating experiences. However, when they first encounter active approaches to learning, such as problem-based learning, they find that their lived experiences, and those of others, are of worth.

Threats to learner identity

Students may have been silenced in lecture-based approaches to learning. In circumstances where students are not allowed to speak or debate, they are often prevented from understanding their own learner identity and epistemological position.

Students who engage with disjunction in a learning environment tend to speak of 'gaining a voice' (Savin-Baden, 2000: 98), as a way to depict an intellectual and ethical process whereby the development of a sense of voice, mind and self are interlinked. The ability to 'construct a voice' (Belenky et al., 1986: 16) encompasses the way in which students speak of engagement with their disjunction and the transitions that often ensue. Constructing a voice is thus a dynamic process through which construction, deconstruction and reconstruction occurs. For example, students may be able to 'speak for themselves' in some circumstances and not others, yet there is not always a conscious realization of voice (or lack of it). Students perhaps are able to speak within their peer group and problem-based learning group, but are not always able to interact with tutors whom they see as experts. For students, the ability to articulate their own confusions around disjunction often results in a shift towards a greater consciousness and/or understanding of their learner identity.

Threshold concepts – a troublesome concept?

Meyer and Land (2003a; 2003b; 2003c) have argued for the notion of a 'threshold concept', the idea of a portal that opens up a way of thinking that was previously inaccessible. Yet there seems to be a certain troublesomeness about the whole idea of threshold concepts. It is interesting that these are defined as 'concepts,' but not as 'knowledge' or 'learning'. It is not entirely clear how they relate to earlier work on 'key concepts' and 'basic concepts'. For example, Kandlbinder and Maufette (2001) examined approaches of teaching 'basic concepts' in science programmes that used student-based learning approaches. Lecturers were first screened to establish whether they had a more learner-focused approach to their teaching than other staff, and in-depth interviews were conducted with these staff. The assumption was that lecturers who were more student-centred would design programmes that would facilitate effective learning. The findings indicate that student-centred teachers in the sciences had the same goals as their less student-centred colleagues, namely, to ensure that students developed a thorough knowledge of the discipline by learning 'basic concepts' at the outset of the course. What was particularly interesting about this study was the foundational view of knowledge, whereby the assumption was that students needed to learn and understand a given body of knowledge, before they could progress to the next level of the course. However, what Kandlbinder and Maufette have argued is that what many lecturers referred to as 'basic concepts', were in fact far from basic. What they appeared to be describing was a pedagogical representation of ecologies of practice. They argued that what emerged from data were four descriptions of what basic concepts were meant to represent to the students. The metaphor of building was central to the notion of disciplinary understanding and knowledge was seen as the ability to test propositions rather than the learning of a body of knowledge through rote memorization. They argued: 'Basic concepts can also form the boundary of received knowledge, providing identity to the discipline. By their nature, these concepts are a particular kind of knowledge that is difficult to locate' (Kandlbinder and Maufette, 2001: 49). The four descriptions they offer of these basic concepts are:

> Pillars: propositions that provide a sound foundation
> Boundaries: contain the knowledge of the discipline
> Web: connects the knowledge of the discipline
> Model: the concepts and their interconnections are tested against reality.

It is not clear whether these concepts are hierarchical but it would seem that they represent an ecology of practice within the science disciplines, which, as Bourdieu has argued, have strongly differentiated power and status, tend to stand in competition with one another, and are 'the locus of competitive struggle' for individual scientists located within the fields. 'What is at stake is the power to impose the definition of science . . . best suited to [individual] specific interests' (Bourdieu, 1975: 23).

The notion of threshold concepts seems to be dislocated from both the learner and the context so that they are seen as generalizable notions of what is troublesome. The result is that in some disciplinary areas the notion of threshold concepts means that they cannot be located differently, even if students' response to them may be different, because of the way they are biographically located. I suggest such generalizability by Land and Meyer is misplaced, and that instead students' understandings of difficulties and different ways of engaging with the concepts and their disjunction are ideas that are more useful. It is important, then, that transitional models such as those presented here need to be both biographically and contextually related.

Scaffolding learning

There remains a strong focus in higher education and particularly in professional education on the notion of scaffolding learning. Emerging from Vygotsky's zone of proximal development (Vygotsky, 1978), it is the distance between the actual developmental level as determined by independent problem-solving and the level of potential development as determined through problem-solving under adult guidance or in collaboration with more capable peers. The concept of scaffolding refers to the context provided by knowledgeable people to help students develop their cognitive skills. There is an increasing focus in higher education on delineating knowledge and teaching experiences for students, resulting in increasingly performative practices. I would suggest that staff's need to scaffold learning is troublesome. There is surely the somewhat hegemonic assumption here that teachers' pedagogical stances are better than those held by their students. Indeed, surely to scaffold is to impose one's own pedagogical signature on the way knowledge is created and managed, instead of enabling and allowing students to use or create their own pedagogical signature. Thus, it might be that staff, through scaffolding, lead students around disjunction and into liminality, thereby only guiding students into transitional states rather than transformative opportunities.

Troublesome power

Troublesome power refers to the idea that not only is power in itself a troublesome concept but also that covert actions associated with particular practices (such as what is allowed and disallowed in a learning context) affect the power plays within the discipline, the learning context and in staff and students' lives. Troublesome power is also seen in the interaction between staff and students in active learning approaches, when 'power to learn' for themselves is offered to the students but what this means in practice is not made explicit. Thus, students who may, for example, construct their own curriculum through seminars often encounter troublesome power later because of the assessment practices that disable their own curriculum construction. The issue of power is rarely openly acknowledged in learning contexts, nor are issues of control and subjectification in general. Lecturers therefore are not only agents of, but also subject to, the disciplinary process of the assessment and measurement of individuals. What is needed instead is a constructivist curriculum in which students can be active, social and creative learners (Perkins, 2006b: 34).

Learning stances

The notion of learning stances, as argued for in Chapter 1, presents learning as complex and specific to the learner, so that it must therefore be located in the context of their lives and their stories. Consequently, the notion of stance is used here to indicate that learners, at different times and in different spaces, 'locate' themselves as a particular learner. Learning stances stand against the notion of learning styles and deep and surface approaches, arguing instead that stances relate not only to cognitive perspectives, but also ontological positioning within learning environments. Thus, conflict between expectation, identity and belief in a learning context can result in staff and students becoming stuck: experiencing disjunction in learning and in teaching, either personally, pedagogically or interactionally.

Challenging dominant narratives

To challenge, question or query the dominant narratives, the status quo, the way things are expected to 'be' in higher education, can result in marginalization, in being a lone or unheard voice, and can also result in a sense of difficulty. Not supplying a bibliography to students, standing against the research assessment exercise or arguing against quality practice would be seen by many academics as being impossible at worst and subversive at best. Yet living and working in and for an uncertain world rather than a performative world can move us into new learning spaces and be a catalyst to personal and pedagogical change.

While the 11 catalysts presented in the preceding pages are only a few of many, it could be said that such catalysts are what Meyer and Land (2006: 26) refer to as 'forms of variation'. However, it would seem that these forms of variation are largely conceptual and bounded in ways that the catalysts delineated here are not.

A model of transitional learning spaces

This model has grown out of my own concerns about the relationship between disjunction and threshold concepts and in particular the (over-) generalizability of such concepts. I would argue that all learning is necessarily biographical and contextually related. Thus this model can only relate to and be shaped by an individual in relation to his or her own stance as a learner.

The model (Figure 7.1) is to be seen as a liquid learning space in which a series of 'learnings' occur. The starting point is a catalyst to change which results in disjunction and movement into a liminal space. However, once through a liminal space the journey continues, over a learning bridge into engagement and on to a position of transition or transformation, then to a place of proactive learning.

Disjunctive spaces

Many staff and students have described disjunction as being a little like hitting a brick wall in learning (see Chapter 5, section entitled 'Disjunctional reflective spaces'). Disjunction is also similar to troublesome knowledge because until it is experienced in a learning environment it is difficult to explain, particularly in terms of students feeling fragmented. After someone has first encountered disjunction they enter a liminal space. However, it might be that there are different types of disjunction or levels of disjunction, and that these might result in movement into different kinds of liminal spaces.

Disjunction is not only a form of troublesome knowledge but also a 'space' or 'position' reached through the realization that the knowledge is

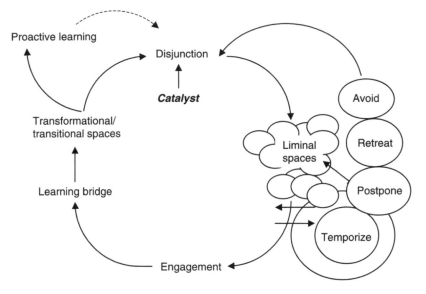

Figure 7.1 A model of transitional learning spaces

troublesome. Disjunction might therefore be seen as a 'troublesome learning space' that emerges when forms of active learning (such as problem-
based learning) are used that prompt students to engage with procedural
and personal knowledge. Alternatively, disjunction can be seen as the kind of
place that students might reach after they have encountered a threshold
concept that they have not managed to breach. Disjunction is thus a form of
troublesome knowledge because it bridges Meyer and Land's (2006) notion
of engagement with troublesome knowledge and the state of liminality. They
suggest that when students find particular concepts difficult they are in a
state of liminality. This state of liminality tends to be characterized by a
stripping away of old identities, an oscillation between states and personal
transformation. However, they suggest that Einstein, when wrestling with the
mathematics of general relativity, may have been in a liminal state in this
possibly apocryphal story presented below:

> Einstein, in a somewhat anxious state, was complaining to Ricci at 'the
> party' about the fact that he was *stuck*. Ricci explained to him what
> tensor calculus could do, and Einstein immediately saw it as the solution
> to his mathematical problems. In fact, tensor calculus became the 'lan-
> guage', or discourse, of general relativity. It is interesting to speculate
> here that Einstein may well have been in a liminal state, temporarily
> suspended by the lack of a formal mathematical vehicle through which
> to express and progress his thinking. (Meyer and Land, 2006: 25, original
> emphasis)

However, I would suggest that Einstein was stuck, he was not in a betwixt and between state but instead had experienced a barrier to moving forward; he was experiencing disjunction. In assisting Einstein, Ricci helped him to move away from his disjunction into a state of liminality – so that liminality was a 'jumping off point' that necessarily follows disjunction – that allowed Einstein, and also allows other people, to begin to see the way forward.

Forms of disjunction

It would seem that it might be possible to locate different forms of disjunctions, although such forms will differ between people, and their encounters with it will vary. However, some of the varieties might include:

A *moment of aporia:*[1] this is where a moment of misconception is drawn attention to by someone else, leaving the person concerned both stuck, exposed and in doubt. For example, at a conference it may become apparent to someone that a concept they believed they had grasped and understood they in fact do not.

A *moment of conceptual puzzlement:* here the self-realization that one is stuck and does not understand how to move on results in a sense of feeling paralysed or fragmented. For example, when grappling with a new idea it may become clear to us that the realization is just under the surface of our thinking, and we realize we are still stuck.

A *cycle of stuckness:* here someone may understand he or she needs to move away from a particular position of stuck space, but not knowing how or where to move to results in a constant cycle of stuckness which leads to a return to the same stuck space repeatedly. For example, in moving from analysing qualitative data to interpreting it, students can just re-analyse the data and create further themes and lists rather that interpreting it at a level of subtext.

A *hermeneutic cycle:* in this form of stuckness revisiting issues and concerns does not result in a cycle of stuckness, but a reconsideration of the issues that have promoted becoming stuck. For example, after reconsidering the difficulties the position of stuckness is seen differently, and the familiar is seen as new or strange. Thus, here there is a sense of reinterpreting what was once familiar and what once seemed whole into a collection of components, some of which are then rendered strange.

The difficulty with disjunction is that explanations of its forms, and possibilities for moving away from them, do not always enable people who are stuck to make the required shift, nor do explanations of stuck spaces necessarily help people to deal with them any better. However, explanations

---

[1] Aporia (Greek: ἀπορία: *impasse, lack of resources, puzzlement, embarrassment*) is a puzzle or an impasse, but it can also denote the state of being perplexed, or at a loss, at such a puzzle or impasse.

concerning what some forms of disjunction might look like for some people is useful in understanding them, particularly since stuckness has a moral element because choosing how to manage it often involves difficult decisions and choices.

Responses to disjunction

Students deal with disjunction in a number of different ways. This means that the conflict, ambiguity and incoherence experienced by individual students cannot be defined by distinctive characteristics, but there are some general trends. What seems to be apparent is that disjunction is dealt with by students, in one of five ways, through forms of decision-making that are conscious and/or unconscious. Thus, students may opt to *retreat* from disjunction, to *postpone* dealing with it, to *temporize* and thus choose not to make a decision about how to manage it, to find some means to *avoid* it and thus create greater disjunction in the long term, or to *engage* with it and move to a greater or lesser sense of integration.

Retreat
In this position, students who experience disjunction choose not to engage with the process of managing it. Here they want to avoid engaging with the struggles connected with disjunction and often retreat behind some form of excuse, which means that they do not engage with the personal or organizational catalyst to the disjunction. Students who retreat may also take up a particular position, entrench themselves within it and then reinforce the bunkers around that position.

Postponement
Students may consider their position of disjunction, invariably because they have experienced disjunction before and learned how to manage it. Thus they choose to postpone movement. This is not a postponement of a decision, as in temporization, but a clear decision to leave this area of learning or life on hold.

Temporizing
Students who do not directly retreat from disjunction may adopt an indecisive or time-serving policy. They not only acknowledge the existence of disjunction, but also that they have to engage with it in order to enable an effective transition to take place, but they decide that it is preferable to postpone making any decision about how to manage it.

Avoidance
In this situation, students do not just temporize but adopt mechanisms that will enable them to find some way of circumventing the disjunction. The result will be that although the student has found a means of bypassing the

disjunction, this may have taken more effort than engaging with it, especially as in the long term, because of the nature of disjunction, they will still have to engage with disjunction in their life world in order to avoid always becoming entrenched in this position.

Note. *Retreat* and *Avoid* can be on the edge of liminality, or within liminality where a position of turning back may occur. *Temporize* and *Postpone* tends to be in the liminal space and the students may stay in these places for some time before engaging.

Engagement

Engaging with disjunction requires that students acknowledge its existence and attempt to deconstruct the causes of disjunction by examining the relationship with both their internal and external worlds. Through this reflexive examination process, students can engage with what has given rise to the disjunction and they are then enabled to shift towards a greater sense of integration.

There is a sense that when people are stuck they tend to retreat to places of safety, places that are known and comfortable. Such spaces are ones in which people feel they can regain control, place boundaries around their stuckness and thereby manage it in some way. As people move towards a catalyst and begin to engage with disjunction, they may retreat to a space of safety, and thus avoid engaging with liminality and the subsequent catalyst out of liminality, thereby preventing movement over a threshold. They may hope that by retreating they will avoid moving into a liminal space, but it is more likely they will locate themselves in a cycle of stuckness. Although this might feel safe, it will actually prevent shifts towards engagement and proactive learning.

Liminal spaces

As mentioned in Chapter 5, the state of liminality tends to be characterized by a stripping away of old identities, an oscillation between states and personal transformation. Liminal spaces are thus suspended states and serve a transformative function, as someone moves from one state or position to another. Engaging with liminal spaces may involve choice, but in the case of troublesome spaces they are often more likely to be stuck spaces, rather than what Ellsworth (1997) has termed 'stuck places'. Ellsworth's conception of stuck places would seem to imply that stuckness is a place one travels to – whereas disjunction is often a position one seems to find oneself in, often somewhat unexpectedly. The term 'stuck spaces' reflects this unexpectedness, their unpredictability and sense of the liminal. Many people know nothing about disjunction before they experience it, so that they enter it unprepared. Maybe because of this, disjunction is where people are at before they reach a liminal space, prompted by a threshold concept or a new learning experience. Thus, having overcome the shock of the disjunction, they find they begin to re-examine their position and, in doing so, see the terrain that they then choose to move through towards a liminal space.

Meyer and Land (2006) argue for preliminal variation but it would seem that what occurs for students is not just 'variation' but different ways of managing the disjunction being experienced. For example, Meyer and Land (2006: 27) believe preliminal variation is a means of distinguishing between 'variation in students' "tacit" understanding (or lack thereof) of a threshold concept'. This, they argue, means that it may be possible to understand why some students approach and manage threshold concepts while others cannot. Yet it might not just be about students' ability to manage the threshold concept, but also their reaction to it. However, I suggest that liminal spaces may be temporary or permanent and sometimes a combination of both, as mentioned in Chapter 5.

Temporary liminal spaces

These are characterized by boundaries in time and space, they are usually:

1. Reflective activities
2. Rites of passage
3. Temporary disjunction.

More or less permanent liminal spaces

These are in a sense liminal states in which one lives, such as the priesthood, serial and long-term travellers and, possibly, serial students and authors.

Transitional and transformational learning spaces

Transitional spaces are places where shifts in learner experience occur, caused by a challenge to the person's life world in particular areas of their lives, at different times and in distinct ways. The notion of transition carries with it the idea of movement from one place to another and with it the necessity of taking up a new position in a different place. Leaving the position and entering transition may also be fraught with difficulties that may result in further disjunction for the student. Thus, transitions can often be difficult and disturbing, and yet simultaneously be areas where personal change takes place. Transformational spaces are spaces where a sense of coming into oneself occurs – there is a sense of identity construction, of self-realization and of seeing the world anew. The difference between transitional and transformational spaces is that in a transitional space there is a sense of shifting from one place to another, whereas in a transformational space there is a sense of life shifts, of knowing the world differently in living, working and learning contexts.

Proactive learning: the beginning and the end of the spiral

The notion of proactive learning is one that requires a new stance, a different vision, an active leap away from previous perspectives. This conception of knowing is the higher-order form of knowing suggested by Perkins (2006a), who has argued for three conceptions of knowing:

1. Retention and application: characterized by ritual type activity such as driving to work
2. Understanding: the ability to perform what you know and thus to be able to think with what you know about, for example, being able to explain causality in history
3. Active and adventurous: a proactive conception of knowledge that requires creativity and the ability to see things differently. This conception requires a leap away from bounded understanding.

While much of the learning that occurs in this model is transitional, the possibilities for transformational learning occur when a leap is made beyond understanding knowledge to engaging with it actively. To engage students in proactive learning, I would suggest, requires engagement with liquid learning and problem situations that prompt students to consider their stances, identities and moral positions.

Learning bridges

Learning bridges vary in their structure and appearance, as well as their perceived relevance by students. Broadly speaking, learning bridges are mechanisms that help to link or connect different past and present positions in ways that enable shifts to be made – whether transitional or transformative. Learning bridges can also be seen as a means of joining issues or positions together and as a means of connecting two unknowns. Further, as Burbules (1997) argues:

> A passage *to* is different from a passage *through*, which is different from a passage *from*. Sometimes a passage connects knowns; sometimes it leads from a known to an unknown. One can differentiate here between the pattern of a constellation, which connects known elements, or givens, and the pattern of a labyrinth, which leads away from the known toward the unknown: in the latter case, *we choose a path, not a destination*. (Original emphasis)

Thus, learning bridges are not merely the connection of two points but are rhizomatic in nature, akin to the way Deleuze and Guattari (1987) describe the World Wide Web, so that learning bridges spread in a number of directions that denote little, if any hierarchy. Learning bridges include:

1. Developing a new position
2. The realization of new modes of knowledge
3. The honing of critique
4. Reviewing prior experiences of learning
5. Legitimating experiences.

Developing a new position

The concept of an epistemological framework captures the idea that following disjunction one is able to take up a new position. Such a position might initially appear to be epistemological, but more often it is both epistemological and ontological. The bridge here is the sense that one is on the way to 'being' different and seeing the world differently.

The realization of new modes of knowledge

Here a shift is made away from knowledge being seen as static, unrelenting or pragmatic. Instead, knowing about people, the virtues of tact and the value of knowledge gaps can all become learning bridges.

The honing of critique

The honing of critique is a learning bridge because it often enables staff and students to see that critique and being critical is not just about negative deconstruction. Through such realization, they begin to see critique as a bridge to other forms of learning and ways of being. Therefore, critique is to be seen as a form of criticism of the discipline (Barnett, 1997). Such a notion of critique brings with it the transcendence of the discipline, and reflexivity around that very transcendence in which differing views are celebrated.

Reviewing prior experiences of learning

Reviewing past experiences of stuck spaces and worthwhile learning can be a learning bridge, since it helps staff and students to recall strategies for progression that may have helped them in the past. Alternatively reviewing can result in an increased possibility of being in a liminal space, because of not finding prior experiences helpful in bridging the current situation. In general, it would seem that reflection on prior experiences does prompt movement away from stuck spaces.

Legitimating experience

Legitimated experience is a learning bridge because it captures the idea that staff learn to value the worth of their experience. It is often through realizing the value of their experience that staff are able to manage disjunction and subsequent transition. Learning bridges are evident in the connections made in the very process of legitimating their own experience. This enables them to acknowledge and interpret the text of their experiences and thus reconstruct prior notions of legitimate forms of learning, knowledge and personal experience.

Conclusion

This chapter has suggested that there needs to be more focus on the contestable nature of knowledge, and the impact of liminal spaces on transforming identities. Further, perhaps there needs to be an engagement with the need for delineating and creating new curriculum spaces, which help students to transcend and manage liminality in ways that embrace contemporary dislocations, locate modes of translation, and mediate rhetoric differently. However, in order to explore this further it is necessary to examine boundary spaces where shifts, liminality and uncertainty are particularly apparent, which are explored in the next chapter.

Part 3

Transforming Locations

8

Boundary Spaces

The notion of boundary spaces captures the idea that there are spaces within civic society, which are in-between spaces, spaces between cultures and politics, between people and institutions and between diverse forms of knowledges. The existence of such boundary spaces introduces questions about how we manage them and what it might mean to live and work at their borders. Borders and in-between spaces are important because it is by understanding these spaces that academics and universities can begin to engage or re-engage with its various publics. In this chapter it is argued that as the university loses spaces – all forms of spaces – it is also losing ground. It is losing ground not only because of the way new forms of activity, working practices and working hours are preventing staff from engaging with dialogic and reflective spaces, but also because it is currently ignoring boundary spaces.

Forms of boundary spaces

The nature and existence of boundary spaces is both challenging and troublesome because they are borderland spaces, spaces where diverse and related concerns both overlap and collide. Collision and overlap occurs in terms of physical positions, customs, cultures and ways of operating. For example, there is often a perception by both employers and university staff that they live and work in separate worlds, and that to go from one to another is almost like passing through the wardrobe into a Narnia world. Such perspectives are endorsed by books by Sinclair (2006) whose title implies that students are not just relocating to a new place, university, but to a new planet. Yet these are not separate worlds but are spaces that have to be managed in relation to one another. Thus, as Engeström suggests (referring to virtual spaces) we have to see the worlds not as Narnia spaces, but more akin to the position in which Harry Potter finds himself, when he has to manage both worlds separately but also in relation to one another (Jones,

2005: 106). Boundary spaces thus overlap and are not just empty spaces of no-man's-land. Boundary spaces are places where cultures collide, partly because different worlds share different values, and they also emerge not just because they are in between but because of issues of perspectives. For example, the way in which we choose to interpret and relate to different worlds from our own can be a barrier to engagement or can instigate the creation of a new learning space.

However, collision and overlap also occur in the boundary spaces at the borders of space creation and space production. Space creation is the process of allowing for flexibility in learning environments and systems. For example, instead of detailed lesson plans, open discussion and student-led learning would be used to create opportunities for reflective and dialogic spaces to emerge. However, what is problematic about space creation is that while it might be possible to create such spaces, the extent to which they result in space production is another matter. Space production is used here to capture the idea that space in a classroom setting is not only used, it is practised; there are gaps for thinking, reflecting and student-led discussion. So space production must be present and students must know that they have space for learning and that they can use these spaces in ways that are important to them. Similarly staff need to know that spaces that they have created for writing and reflection are seen as valid spaces by the leadership of the university, so that they can be productive spaces and not interrupted spaces or patrolled spaces.

As mentioned in previous chapters, higher education worldwide in the early 2000s is becoming increasingly performative and patrolling. National agenda in the UK and Australia that focus on quality assurance and research assessment are some of the more obvious manifestations of this, but it can also be seen in the delimitation of risk and the increase in rules governing academic life. For example, it is expected by many university managers that the imposition of staff and students' charters will produce better behaved students and academics. Furthermore, keys and passwords in university life increasingly limit freedom and access to what should be seen as civic spaces, such as university campuses, buildings and libraries. The idea that civic spaces can be patrolled best by controlling movement and limiting access illustrates that spaces such as these are seen as products where risk must be minimized, disruptive intervention avoided and the possibility limited of construction of new civic spaces. Yet at the same time, institutions such as the Massachusetts Institute of Technology in the USA and the Open University in the UK have removed passwords to their Internet sites, in order to create the possibilities of more open civic spaces. In contrast, the open source spaces of wikis are now being overtaken by closed wikis, hidden behind university (virtual) doors, which minimize risk, and reduce the possibility of some untoward comments being open to the public gaze. The growth in these risk-averse stances in academic life means that boundary spaces are being both ignored and controlled. As long as it is possible to measure, control or regulate it, issues can be safe and manageable to the institution. Yet such approaches close down the possibilities for engaging with new forms of knowledge, diverse ways of operating and new ways of being and learning in academic life.

Cultural boundaries

Cultural boundaries are evident in spaces where programmes have been transplanted from one culture to another. Many universities have outreach campuses in their own country but in different types of communities from those created by a university campus. However, what is becoming increasingly prevalent is the location of a UK campus overseas, where students who attend the university are those who have learned how to learn in a different way from those who have experienced UK schooling. Yet questions remain as to how academics manage the differences and challenges that emerge from working at such boundaries. How do they import a campus without imperialism, and how do they come to know and understand how students in that country know and understand their worlds? It is suggested here that to date there is relatively little research and understanding about the ways in which universities engage with their overseas partners. An example would be a transcultural programme; the delivery of a programme, either at a distance or face to face, to students located in a different country, where the offering institution largely supports and adapts the programme. Such programmes are increasingly common but there are many issues that need careful consideration, such as how students consider the authority and credibility of staff, how that affects their readiness to question and debate with staff, and wider issues of beliefs, values and attitudes about ethics, illness and health care, cultural religious traditions and the like. Further, it would seem vital to tailor the creation of learning spaces and knowledge production to the specific cultural context of the students, even though some tutors may suggest, with Biggs (1999), that cultural difference can be overcome by applying universal principles of good teaching, regardless of where the programme is taught. These spaces need to be different cultural spaces where the cultures of all are *regarded* and the mere pretence of regard is not tolerated.

University boundaries

University boundaries are not just related to the forms of knowledge and types of disciplinary area with which one particular university chooses to engage. It is more fundamental than this and relates to the spaces which the university chooses to inhabit or shun. For example, the UK higher education system has become increasingly stratified. It was felt by some (Trow, 1974) that the loss of the binary line between polytechnics and universities in 1992 would result in less stratification. Yet with the introduction and continuance of activities such as the research assessment exercise in the UK, and more recently in Australia, stratification is increasing and solid knowledge proliferates, the higher up the university is ranked. Thus, in the current solid and performative culture many universities are attempting to reinvent and regenerate themselves in order to survive the stratification. This can be seen emerging in the form of striated and solid modernity, and the clinging on to knowledge values on the one hand and a shift towards a performative enterprise culture on the other. Both staff and students dislike such polarized perspectives – those who teach and experience solid knowledge are tending to leave. For example, in 2006 a top-ranked UK university experienced both a low-scoring student satisfaction survey and staff disaffection, resulting in many moving to other local universities. What is needed instead is a reconceptualization of knowledge – so that knowledge is seen as smooth liquid not solid striation.

However, within universities there are also boundary spaces such as the spaces between students' expectations and conceptions of learning and those of the staff – and the space between the experiences of both. Work by Trigwell et al. (1999) and more recently Trigwell and Ashwin (2006) indicate that qualitatively different approaches to teaching are associated with different responses to learning. While earlier work by Trigwell et al. (1999) argued for five qualitatively different approaches to teaching, it is the relationship between such approaches and students' conceptions of learning that illustrates the boundary space here. For example, Trigwell and Ashwin (2006) suggest there is variation in students' and teachers' conceptions of academic tasks, which in turn is related to the quality of teaching and learning experienced by teachers and students. Further, they suggest that this variation not only exists within each of these groups but also between teachers and students. However, what is absent from these studies is an exploration of what occurs at the borders of what teachers espouse and what they do in practice, although it would seem some of the work based on explorations of the Oxford University tutorial system are beginning to engage with this debate. Ashwin (2005) suggests four qualitatively different ways are evident in the way in which students and teachers experience tutorials:

1. Tutorials as a place where tutors help students to develop an understanding of concepts
2. Tutorials as a place where students see how to approach their discipline
3. Tutorials as a place where evidence is critically discussed
4. Tutorials as a place where new positions on the topic are developed and refined.

However, there remains relatively little exploration of students' conceptions of learning, their experience of learning and their actual study habits.

A further university boundary space is between student learning and the learning context. For some staff, tapping keyboards, texting and looking out of the window are seen as interruptions to learning. Similarly, noisy libraries and discussion occurring around computers are also seen as spaces that hinder learning. Yet for many students the ability to think and multitask is a space that many continually inhabit. Thus to prevent the use of laptops in classrooms, to turn off the wireless network and to build lecture theatres without windows are closing down the multiple learning spaces that many of the net generation value most.

Membership boundaries

The notion of membership boundaries captures the idea that within a civic society there are often powerful boundaries, such as the school gates. Late twentieth century decades have brought with them a shift away from strict boundaries, towards the creation of theme parks, shopping malls and, in particular, holiday spaces ranging from Butlins to Centre Parcs. These have resulted in a series of interrelated simulacra whereby fiction and reality merge. From being a 'member' of the Co-op supermarket of the 1960s to possessing a larger supermarket's loyalty card today, presents a situation whereby now 'membership' is equated with commitment to spending in particular ways and in particular places. With the use of barcodes the subtext of the notion of loyalty is more related to the shopper providing information about spending habits in order to allow the supermarket to market their products ever more effectively. Thus, the erosion of membership boundaries in areas such as the university is becoming increasingly problematic since lack of commitment to a notion of membership often results in reduced commitment and increased blame towards the organizations. To buy into membership usually means loyalty and commitment to a culture and a way of operating, but the slipping away of membership has resulted in rebranding and reinvention by many universities, in order to attempt to regain ground – not just in terms of gaining student numbers but also in order to create commitment and a sense of belonging.

Civic boundaries

Although there has been discussion about civic spaces, the issue of civic boundaries is one that remains both contested and largely neglected in the context of higher education. Civic spaces have been defined in various ways, particularly in relation to human geography and social capital, but they are defined here as spaces 'in which people of different origins and walks of life can co-mingle without over-control by government, commercial or other private interests, or *de facto* dominance by one group over another' (Douglas, 2002: 2). For Douglas, civic spaces reach beyond the realms of public spaces and are therefore seen as being located in broader ethereal spaces – such as private or nominally private spaces that might include cafés, pubs, parks and even, possibly, supermarkets. However, the concern here is with civic boundaries, boundaries at which universities and academics increasingly work. Civic boundaries constitute the boundaries between the academic community and its various publics: business, government, not-for-profit sectors and students. In many ways, the notion of civic boundaries is an overarching concept under which many of the boundary spaces discussed in the chapter are located. However, what is particularly important about the concept of civic boundaries is that it is in these diverse spaces of interaction with its publics that issues of values, language, trust and judgement collide. For example, the increased accountability of university to government agenda, along with increased 'cultural suspicion' (O'Neill, 2002) has resulted in not only inconsistency but also confusion of role and purpose:

> *In theory* the new culture of accountability and audit makes professionals and institutions more accountable *to the public.* This is supposedly done by publishing targets and levels of attainment in league tables, and by establishing complaint procedures by which members of the public can seek redress for any professional or institutional failures. But underlying this ostensible aim of accountability *to the public* the real requirements are for accountability *to regulators, to departments of government, to funders, to legal standards.* The new forms of accountability impose forms of central control – quite often indeed a *range of different and mutually inconsistent* forms of central control. (O'Neill, 2002: 52–3, emphases added)

Reid (1996) poses the question of 'higher education or education for hire?': the university of the early 2000s is on shifting sands. The increasingly striated and stratified university sector is trying to rebuild itself amid the surrounding forces of civic disengagement, marketization and pernicious ideologies that threaten its very being and purpose.

It is noticeable that as broken societies rebuild themselves after war or disaster the focus tends to be less on government, although there is often some attempt at this, and more on institutions such as hospitals, schools and places of community shelter. There is a tendency for humankind to focus on re-creation of community spaces in order to rebuild society, rather than to focus on law and order. Yet it is in the boundary spaces of personal institutional life that civic disengagement is also seen. Civic disengagement is often seen as being characterized by the decline of voter participation and community volunteering. Macfarlane (2005) notes that there are many explanations offered for this, which include modern working practices, labour mobility, the 24-hour consumer society and the breakdown of the nuclear family. Yet Macfarlane also suggests that civic disengagement can be seen creeping into academic life and: 'that the erosion of academic self-governance has led to the decline of political literacy in academic life and that a range of other forces, including under-funded massification and research audits, have damaged social and moral responsibility and the responsibilities implied by community involvement' (Macfarlane, 2005: 296).

However, it also possible to see that universities themselves are changing the nature of civic engagement, through not only university course provision seven days a week from 8 a.m. to 11 p.m., but also through changing the nature of volunteering. For example, some universities have student volunteer schemes, partly to encourage civic engagement but also to improve the link between the university and the local community. Yet having set up student volunteering schemes, some universities are then accrediting them – so volunteering becomes a marketable product and an asset to individualism, rather than a moral responsibility and a commitment to the good of the community. Some authors have argued that the university is in ruins (Readings, 1997), others (Barnett, 2003) have suggested the university needs to be reinvented, still others that the academic ethic has to be regained (Dill, 2005).

Dill suggests that it is important that academics not only critique the impact of market forces and government intervention on higher education, but also that the academic community itself engages with the faults that this has created. In order to retain academics' autonomy, he argues, not only must academic standards be rigorous but there needs to be re-engagement with the notion of the academic ethic. For Dill, the academic ethic refers to the standards and behaviours that govern academic standards and guide our choices as academics. In short, we must engage with professional self-regulation in terms of the impact we, as academics have on social and political behaviour. Yet if as academics we live with chronic uncertainty and identities on the move, self-regulation and standards also become contestable spaces. Perhaps what needs to be recognized, then, is the importance of pedagogic identity. Bernstein (1992) has argued that through their experiences as students, individuals within higher education are in the process of identity formation. He has suggested that this process may be seen as the construction of pedagogic identities, which will change according to the different relationships that occur between society, higher education and knowledge. Pedagogic identities are defined as those that 'arise out of contemporary culture and technological change that emerge from dislocations, moral, cultural, economic and are perceived as the means of regulating and effecting change' (Bernstein, 1992: 3). Thus, pedagogic identities are characterized by the emphases of the time. In the traditional disciplines of the 1960s students were inducted into the particular pedagogical customs of those disciplines. Pedagogic identities of the 1990s were characterized by a common set of market related, transferable skills. Haggis argues that different 'types' of student motivation in higher education, such as motivation related to work and employment, are often seen to be less valuable that 'love of learning' or vice versa. Thus this 'suggests the possibility of a more complex and interconnected set of pressures, reactions and desires, within which learning at university appears, for some students at least, to present possibilities for the creation of new identities and selves' (Haggis, 2004: 350).

It would seem that higher education allows for the preparation for, or production of, particular identities and therefore necessarily prevents the development of others. If universities are to become more inclusive they need to move away from knowledge practices that promote individualistic notions of knowledge development, towards the idea of knowledge creation communities. Perhaps then, the pedagogic identities of the 2000s are to be characterized by the juxtaposition of liminality and uncertainty with performativity and enterprise.

Yet if such reinvention is really to take place, the university needs to engage with boundary spaces. Macfarlane (2005) argues that civic disengagement is pervading academic life because academics are no longer prepared to engage in university decision-making, supporting colleagues and communicating with the public. Dill argues for new forms of professional regulation through cross-faculty-led peer review, rewarding new processes that improve academic standards with financial incentives. However, he also suggests the development of university-wide marking standards that is an approach already adopted by many universities worldwide. Although such systems have helped both staff and students to understand and utilize grading systems more effectively than formerly, university and even faculty-wide systems have resulted in the papering over of disciplinary differences and cultures.

Disciplinary boundaries

Disciplinary differences remain and the boundary spaces between them should be explored rather than ignored. To communicate about differences at disciplinary borders is important to both the notion of academic ethics and for academic citizenship. Until we have understood other disciplines within the faculty in which we work, effective and transparent peer review systems and successful teaching innovation is unlikely to occur. Disciplinary differences are here to stay and can be seen not only in academic life, but also in the boundary spaces where work-based learning, academic disciplines, class cultures and perceptions of learning collide. For example, the film *Educating Rita* tells the story of hairdresser Rita who is undertaking a part-time Open University degree. During this film she is asked to defend her essay by her tutor, Frank:

> Frank: I want to talk about this that you sent me.
> Rita: That? Oh!
> Frank: Yes. In response to the question, 'Suggest how would you resolve the staging difficulties inherent in a production of Ibsens's *Peer Gynt*' you have written, quote 'Do it on the radio', unquote.
> Rita: Precisely.
> Frank: Well?
> Rita: Well what?
> Frank: Well, I know it's probably quite naive of me but I did think you might let me have a considered essay.
> Rita: That's all I could do in the time . . .
> Frank: But you can't go on producing work as thin as this . . .
> Rita: . . . But I thought it was the right answer.
> Frank: It's the basis for an argument, Rita, but one line is hardly an essay.
> Rita: . . . I sort of encapsulated all of my ideas into one line.
> Frank: But it's not enough.

Rita: Why not?

Frank: It just isn't.

Later

Frank: What?

Rita: I've done it.

Frank: You've done it?

Frank (reading aloud): 'In attempting to resolve the staging difficulties in a production of Ibsen's *Peer Gynt* I would present it on the radio because as Ibsen himself says, he wrote the play as a play for voices, never intending it to go on in a theatre. If they had the radio in his day that's where he would have done it. (Russell, 1983)

To understand what counts as an essay, an assessment or a seminar in different disciplines and universities is a boundary space, a space that requires dialogic translation. If we are to have professional self-regulation and embrace academic citizenship, it will be vital to be able to live and work in disciplinary boundary spaces. However, there is hope. Dialogue is taking place in new spheres and diverse arena: at the boundaries of knowledge, at the borders of knowledge status and values and in new boundary spaces.

Dialogic translation captures the idea that through dialogue staff and students are able to understand new and different languages and conceptions through discussion. In terms of the students' perspective, the understanding of module guides and assessment procedures are often forms of written communication that confuse students. Yet it is in their discussions of what is required and of developing a shared understanding that they are able to translate the information into something that is meaningful and useful to them. For example Emma, a university lecturer in an area of health sciences, explained her experience of being a student on an inter-professional Master's module in Learning and Teaching. Her reflection captures many of the feelings and concerns raised by students and staff, whether undergraduate or postgraduate, about how they learn to understand the languages of higher education:

> The first few weeks were like being in a new job or moving house (in a different country too!). The shock of the language was there – was I in the wrong group? I only had vague understandings. The tears of frustration flowed and I slipped into the wallowing of self-pity. However looking around I was not alone, others were sinking into the depths of despair questioning why we were doing this especially as we were paying too! Time is a great healer so I am told and indeed it would be true to say that some 6 months after the course I can see what has happened to me. I have been transformed in to a . . . Yes the course did finish but I am still growing, developing and changing. I did pass and that did matter although I was not at all bothered by the mark. At the end of the day what was it all about? I realised that the module tutors were not there to test me but to develop me, challenge my thinking and expand me generally. Yes I started out feeling inadequate, inferior, low self-esteem and

believing that I could not write anything of value. Now? Well, I feel positive about myself. I still feel at the bottom of the rung but then I realise that we probably all do!

The idea that disciplines have a new language, different from other languages, we may or may not have learned. Tears, fears and laughter are all part of learning and managing knowledge, and are matters that many of us already experience. However, we may not actually have time to explain disciplinarity and organizational language differences to each other or to our students. These forms of dialogic translation are complex for staff and students because they are connected with shifts in identity for both, but there are principles that can be applied across context and disciplines. Thus as Burbules has argued:

> Teachers need to help learners not by giving them maps, but by helping them to learn how to create maps, to draw lines and make connections themselves. Teaching in this latter sense is not a process of conversion, but of translation: of making sufficient associations between the familiar and the foreign to allow the learner to make further associations, to find other paths, and eventually to become a translator, a path-maker, on their own. Learning how to ask a good question is in one sense *the* central educational task, yet one that is almost never taught explicitly, and rarely taught at all. The typical sorts of questions teachers ask are questions to which the teacher already knows the answer. (Burbules, 1997)

Thus despite the increasingly contestable nature of knowledge and the moving back and forth that increasingly occurs across disciplinary boundaries, disciplines continue to remain a means of ordering and organizing academic work, practices and cultures. The consequence is that academics, as well as students, need maps in order that there is greater understanding of the diversity of disciplinary landscapes.

Employer boundaries

There is a sense, then, that knowledge can be seen as a set of goods placed before the students, and students' perceptions of what counts as knowledge therefore relates very strongly to what staff present as being knowledge. Thus although students may be asked to take a stance towards knowledge, rarely are they asked to deconstruct the extent to which it should be seen as knowledge or to consider why it is seen by the lecturer as acceptable or valid knowledge. Further, there continues to be controversy at the boundaries of Mode 1 knowledge and Mode 2 knowledge; what is considered by many employers as knowledge for the work place. For example, in the UK, the fact that health service managers demand that they are the decision-makers regarding learning and knowledge, because they fund university places, is both troubling and problematic. This is because to define graduate knowledge as that which enables students to be equipped by competence to practise as a nurse, doctor or physiotherapist is to downgrade not only the purpose of the university but also the nature of reading for a degree. While the relationship between learning and work has been a complex arena for some years, the debates relating to different forms of work-based learning seem to have become increasingly contested concepts. For example, Cairns and Stephenson (2002) suggested it might be best understood as learning for, at or through work. Thus, learning for work usually involves work placements on sandwich degrees or professional programmes where students experience the realities of the work setting. Learning at work is characterized by staff training initiatives provided in-house which are rarely formally assessed or accredited. Whereas learning through work involves the negotiation of a programme of study tailored to meet the needs of the learner and their own work context. However, with the growth and emphasis on service learning, the boundaries between the diverse types of work-based learning are becoming increasingly muddled. Service learning encapsulates the idea that learning in diverse and complex practice settings equip students to assess problems, design and implement interventions, and deal with emotions arising from what they see. In short it is:

> a strategy through which students engage with a community so they learn and develop together through organised service that meets mutually identified needs. Service learning helps foster civic responsibility through coordinated activity with a higher education institution and a community. It is an integral part of the academic curriculum (which may be credit-bearing) and includes structured time for role-players (students, community, higher education institution and others) to reflect on the service experience and modify actions if indicated. (Lorenzo et al., 2006: 276–7)

However, what is also important about service learning is that students negotiate the nature of the involvement they have with communities. Thus, learning in such practice settings ensures that civic engagement occurs, because of the commitment to negotiation with community groups, organizations and other stakeholders. Thus, such boundary working results in learning spaces whereby communities and students learn and promote change together.

What is interesting about the interrelationship between learners, universities and employers is that although the boundaries between them have become increasingly contested, there remain difficulties. For example, many employers argue that they require graduates who can problem-solve and think for themselves, but at the same time argue for curricula that are practical, work-based and rely on students being 'trained' for a job. The boundary problems here are in understanding not only the purpose of higher education, but also what it can offer to students and employers. Training for a particular occupation is a short-sighted stance as Stenhouse (1975) suggested. This was discussed earlier in Chapter 2.

Boundary grief

Grief is a boundary space because it is a space of loss but also, in the case of learning, it may be seen as a space of renewal and rebuilding. Perry (1981) has argued for the practice of 'allowing for grief' in the process of growth and development in learning. However, such spaces can be painful and difficult to inhabit, and have personal cost in terms of leaving old lives and perspectives behind. As a result of this there is often a sense of grief and loss after moving out of or away from transformational spaces. For example, work on the stages of grief developed by Kubler-Ross (1973) in the context of death and dying are often mirrored when emerging from a transformation, or following an identity shift:

- *Denial* – here there is an immediate realization of moving towards a liminal space and the possibility of a number of losses. Students deny the possible impact of the learning on their identity, both as a learner and in life as a whole.
- *Anger* – here the students feel fragmented and seek to blame tutors for the position of transition in which they find themselves, often questioning their place on the course and the methods of teaching used that have promoted such losses.
- *Bargaining* – in this stage students seek some kind of truce with the tutor, thus they may seek considerable support, help with assignments and interventions in complex group discussions, rather than seeking to manage the situation themselves.
- *Depression* – the students feel depressed because they feel they have little control over the transition they are experiencing. This, for many students, is a stage of feeling acute stuckness and here they often become inert, not knowing how to move forward.
- *Acceptance* – at this stage the students face the transition calmly. They may have to continue to live with feeling stuck for a while, or they may move out of being stuck into a time of renewal and celebration, and discover ways of managing their new identities.

Thus, in allowing for grief it will be possible for staff to help students to acknowledge and come to terms with their sense of loss. Yet students will need to be helped to take further steps towards transcending their knowing and encouraged to develop new meanings in order that they are prevented from slipping towards disjunction, isolation and alienation. If educators can offer students space for learning and for managing their grief in the transitional process then transitions can be managed, not necessarily without pain or loss, but at least with meaningful and realistic support that helps students to legitimize their experiences.

However, experiencing grief is also something that affects staff, particularly when more interactive forms of learning are used, that result in loss of power and control for staff. Yet engaging with the grief often brings with it the realization that the loss brings greater freedom for students and a broader view of learning and knowledge creation for staff. Grief is a boundary space because it challenges both staff and students' conceptions of knowledge and teaching. The trauma of grief often emerges through the loss of comfort and familiarity with particular approaches to teaching. Acceptance comes as staff realize that shifts in learner identity and their own pedagogical stances are vital spaces of transition and transformation.

Conclusion: new boundary spaces?

Much of what appears to be occurring in many universities in the early 2000s, in the UK at least, is an avoidance of in-depth dialogue in new public spaces, spaces such as work place learning and service learning. It is almost as if the enterprise debate overlaid with performativity has prevented dialogue from taking place in new public spaces. What is needed instead is a review of such spaces, a casting out of old forms of enterprise and performativity, and instead a creation of new boundary spaces where new languages of higher education, commerce, business, industry and health services can debate using shared voices and stances. Thus, if the university is going to claim new spaces in a liquid society (a society characterized by movement, flow and shifting boundaries) it needs to consider what universities might look like in the future, and how different types of universities might relate to their various publics. Yet how might such a university be created and what might this mean in terms of the relationship with its publics? Barnett (2003) has suggested the need to engage with truthfulness, abandon epistemology and engage with each other, hold ideologies with ideologies and develop and use new spaces. Yet it would seem that it is the boundary spaces that remain important sites of opportunity, so they must be valued and used. Such openness will lead to the emergence of new boundary spaces and dialogue, new spaces in-between, where criticality, debate and deliberative democracy can grow and flourish.

9

Spatial Identities

Introduction

The focus in this chapter is not only on how academics portray themselves in digital spaces but also the changes that occur to identity in new learning spaces. This section draws on research into how changes occur in academic identity through engaging in new and re-created learning spaces that are not merely about the location of identities in cyberspaces, but capture the sense that identities are continually under construction and that they change and shift in diverse and often dislocated learning spaces. Thus, the concept of spatial identities captures the idea of identities being spatial; they are on the move in ever shifting spaces, they are essentially ungraspable. This ungraspability relates to the way in which identities differ and change according to context, culture, role and identity. Therefore, what identities mean in the context of learning games differs from those that emerge in textual spaces and will have different qualities, although there may be some overlap. This chapter attempts to help us to grasp and understand such identity positions and locate ways of managing them in the changing terrain of higher education. Thus, this chapter examines how we contend with our changed and changing identities in learning spaces in ways that enhance our lives as individuals as well as participants in academic communities.

Situating spatial identities

Identity, particularly in academic life, is always something that seems to be on the move. Further, the notion of spatial identities is in danger of being conjured up as something with celestial qualities. Yet through understanding our spatial identities it may be possible to map the ways in which we might constitute ourselves as academics, might engage in these diverse spatial zones and might find means of reconstituting our practice, so that it reflects the complex spatialities in which we work. Yet capturing these spatial identities is troublesome, nettlesome even. This is because to argue for the reformulation of our identities and for re-creating spaces in academic life is utopian at one level, since it requires not only the reformulation of the academic role but also a reconstitution of the notion of higher education. Thus the question that transcends *being* an academic and *having* a higher education system is not just about understanding the purpose of higher education, but how it might be re-engaged with, in order that learning spaces might be recaptured so that we can live and work in a reconstituted system. As such, it is important to recognize that learning spaces differ and change at different points on our academic journey. Yet it is also possible that by not using learning spaces, or by continually inhabiting striated learning spaces, identities can become noxious and troubled as other people instigate the management of our lives.

The concept of spatial identities captures the idea that while we have different roles and identities, the places in which they collide, the liminal spaces, enable us to create new and differently formed identities that emerge out of these liminal spaces. These spatial identities can be ignored or developed, but for many people it is through the development of spatial identities in smooth, though not necessarily unproblematic spaces, that transformation tends to occur. In order to allow for the creation of spatial identities it is important that our striated spaces do not become increasingly overpopulated – an example of this can be seen on the Outlook diary, where other people may be given (or even take) the right to manage our diary and thus our spaces. The perception is often that if a space is not 'filled' it should be, and that others have the right to fill it on our behalf. Yet at the same time, it is important that in claiming our own space we must not set ourselves against one another in a Balkanized kind of fashion. Rather, it is important to ensure our spaces are secure but also to realize that such nomadic space is a complex but stimulating place to inhabit. Thus, spatial identities relate to the emergence of new, conflicting forms of embodiment in higher education, not just in terms of role change and role difference but also in relationship to liminal identities.

Liminal identities

Liminal identities are the identity formations that occur in liminal spaces and states. While it seems that the notion of a liminal identity is not really a possibility because liminality is a betwixt and between state, the literature relating to liminality would seem to indicate that within liminal states there are in fact phases or positions of transition. Liminal identities, then, are those that occur with/in liminal spaces, whether one has the old identity or the new. Thus to some extent the transitions experienced in liminal states are of movement towards unknown destinations and unknown identities. This liminal identity is a transitional process that involves the sloughing off of the old identity with the new one in sight.

An example of this is provided by Mandela describing his own experience of the Xhosa rite of passage into manhood, which requires payment by animals, whisky and money. In his biography Mandela speaks of the rituals, where after the circumcision ceremony in which he was declared a man, he returned to the hut: 'We were now *abakwetha*, initiates into the world of manhood. We were looked after by an *amakhankatha*, or guardian, who explained the rules we had to follow if we were to enter manhood properly' (Mandela, 1994: 33). Mandela then describes a series of rituals and ceremonies which were rules he had to follow. Clearly the position in which Mandela found himself after circumcision was a liminal space; although declared a man, this was the space in which he was located before he would enter manhood properly. This rite of passage still remains a vital (if expensive) tradition for Xhosa men, and is a tradition that has not yet been questioned through the South African transformation agenda. In terms of the costs of liminal spaces in academic life, many academics verbalize stories about liminal identities in the context of the personal costs of both undertaking a PhD and the experience of their viva. Thus it can be seen that the transition through liminality brings with it not only new knowledge and understanding for the participating individual, but also new status and identity within the community.

Socially sanctioned liminality and transgressive forms of liminality

It would appear that some forms of formulations of liminality are more acceptable than others. For example, the rituals and associated liminality Turner describes seem to be those that are socially sanctioned, and that seek to maintain the status quo:

> Both these types of ritual [i.e. status elevation and reversal] reinforce structure. In the first, the system of social position is not challenged. The gaps between the positions, the interstices, are necessary to the structure. If there were no intervals, there would be no structure, and it is precisely the gaps that are reaffirmed in this kind of liminality. The structure of the whole equation depends on its negative as well as its positive signs. (Turner, 1969: 201)

Examples of socially sanctioned liminality would be entry into a profession through graduation, becoming a married person through a ceremony, or changing social status. An issue that appears to be discussed little in relation to the recent interest in liminality (for example, Meyer and Land, 2006; Sibbett, 2006) is the relationship between liminality and ritual in academic contexts. It would seem that although there is some acknowledgement that engaging with threshold concepts relates to the rites of passage of becoming a professional, the rituals associated with these rites are somewhat obfuscated. Much of the work on liminality to date has been based on rituals and rites of passage, whether becoming a man, a priest or a cancer patient.

However, unacceptable forms of liminality also exist and invariably seem to emerge in symbolic expressions that are seen to be disruptive or transgressive. Such forms tend to be oppositional in nature, characterized, for example, by not being involved in traditional and often patriarchal ceremonies, as Tambiah argues:

> Ritual is a culturally-constructed system of symbolic communication. It is constituted of patterned and ordered sequences of words and acts, often expressed in multiple media, whose content and arrangement are characterised in varying degrees by formality (conventionality), stereotyping (rigidity), condensation (fusion), and redundancy (repetition). (Tambiah, 1985: 128)

Thus movements away from liminal spaces tend to be celebrated differently and are often seen as being eccentric, for example, choosing not to graduate following a PhD but instead to make a quilt with friends, or carrying out a peace ceremony at home to celebrate the resolution of a difficult and troublesome conflict. Such rituals or symbolic expressions are therefore often hidden or have been moved into hidden spaces. As a result these rituals are often marginal and seen as subversive since they are seen to stand against rites of passage, rituals and liminality as a form of social control. Thus, it might be that liminality could be seen as ultimately hegemonic because it is used to maintain rituals and the status quo – or might it be that it is the ritualizing practices that bring about liminality that in themselves are necessarily hegemonic?

The place and spaces of ritual and ritualization are often conflictual spaces, but it is not entirely clear what the place of conflict is in ritual and liminal spaces – Turner, for example, seems to suggest that rituals are a means of 'containing' conflict. It might be that threshold concepts themselves are hegemonic in higher education, for example, if a student does not engage with them and the (new) rituals associated with them, then students may risk transgressing the rituals and social practices of the discipline. Thus the keenness exhibited in the recent literature (for example, chapters in Meyer and Land, 2006) for 'embedding' threshold concepts in curricula in an epistemic way, has little ontological understanding of the fact that to do so might be seen as creating or affirming a dominant narrative and as a means of ritualizing disciplinary practice. Thus it might not be possible to 'become' an engineer, lawyer or economist unless the student has passed over a number of given knowledge thresholds. Therefore is it possible to begin to locate different types of threshold, such as ritual, epistemic and narrative. These may not be merely liminal identities that are emerging, but instead threshold identities – they are identities that occur and emerge as one is passing out of a liminal space and over the threshold – but the position one finds one's self in the specific action of crossing the threshold retains some of the hallmarks and vestiges of liminality located in the threshold identity.

Textual identities

Textual identities are broadly defined as those that utilize text in some forms to portray or to project identities. Commonly textual identities are seen as those of the authorial voice in monographs or journal articles. However, the increasing use of electronic text – whether email, blog or hypertext – has promoted shifts in views about ways in which textual identities are perceived. In particular, hypertext may be seen as a form of spatial identity as it challenges notions of static and gendered identities.

Hypertext is a way of organizing material that attempts to overcome the inherent limitations of traditional text and in particular its linearity. However, hypermedia is probably a more useful definition for the early 2000s, since this is a medium in which diverse media such as hyperlinks, text and graphics are combined to create a non-linear medium of information. For many educationalists hypertext has been used because through it students can be encouraged to develop levels of criticality – so they are not just covering material but are making connections, both 'clicking' connections and epistemological ones. Landow (1997) offers an interesting approach and some provocative perspectives, that suggest that using hypertext assessments encourages students to engage with complexity and to develop positions of contestability. Yet it is questionable as to whether, in a modular system, students have the requisite time to spend on hypertext, and the fact that these forms of assessment are not being used more extensively in higher education might suggest that this is the case.

Yet, given the increasing sophistication of the wiki, the relationship between a hypertext project and a wiki would seem to be becoming an increasingly contestable space. However, what is particularly interesting about these textual spaces, for example, the Soyinka web (a project involving students in the collaborative production of hypertext [Landow, 1997] and its later iterations), is that there is a striking shift in the relationship between writer and reader, academics and students, academic textual voices and new formulations of academic voices emerging from students. Yet what is also interesting is the way in which hypertext tends to take the 'form of appropriation and abrupt juxtaposition' (Landow, 1997: 251), something that becomes apparent in a number of hypertext sites (see, for example, Streeter et al., 2002). This interruption of assumptions and use of juxtaposition to challenge and create challenge seems to be something we have lost, or maybe not have even had, over the past ten years in higher education. Students of the new millennium, it would seem, just want to get through the course and do the assessment, it is almost as if *really* being challenged takes up too much time and costs too much. Yet, as discussed in Chapter 6, 'Digital Spaces', the relationships between literacy and electracy introduce some interesting issues, particular in the context of ideas such as mystory. For example, Ulmer (2003) asks his students to focus their learning around a particular subject position (family, career, entertainment, history) in order to create story. Thus, the focus is on identity transformation rather than just pedagogical transformation, which would seem also to be the focus of other forms of learning.

A further example of this kind of identity transformation can be seen in projects such as trAce, an online writing project (Thomas, 2005). This project has hosted a series of online writing projects that present snapshots of every-day life. These 'texts' comprise confessionals, inscriptions and memorials; small components of peoples' stories presented as a form of open source perspective on lives. Projects such as this create a sense of being unfamiliar with much of life because of the creative reflections inherent in people's stories. Such projects seem to expose blogs and wikis as being almost tired or even passé and yet are fascinating and disturbing digital spaces fraught with possibilities. Nevertheless it could be argued that wiki environments such as SnipSnap offer similar possibilities, for example Bayne has suggested that in the Romantic Audience Project 'the distinction between content, communi-cation and assessment is creatively undermined – the communicative form is itself the content of the course' (Bayne, 2005b: 12).

A further issue and discussion regarding hypertext writing and projects is the question of authorship. In an age where writing for publication is demanded by management, collaborative hypertext projects and the loss of authorial voices entailed in locating oneself in such spaces introduces inter-esting ethical questions about ownership. One might assume that many of those people involved in these kinds of projects would be submitting their work for the research assessment exercise (RAE) as some kind of installation rather than as a solid piece of text. Yet it remains important, in this post-modern world, to continue to question notions of authorial self. There remain assumptions by many academics that a coherent authorial self exists (which of us is ever coherent?), yet this begins to introduce questions about the possibility of gaining a writer identity and a writing voice.

Patched identities

The notion of patched identities captures the idea that in the process of writing and particularly for novice writers of *learning* to write, a situation emerges whereby the writer identity is in transition. Here there is an overlay-ing of multiple identities as novice writers locate themselves amid, with and often through the voices of those being used as sources for the text being written. This is often seen as plagiarism in students, but is actually more complex than a process of stealing the words or the work of others, instead this is termed patchwriting and results in a patchwork of other identities being used to formulate what is being written.

The concept of patchwriting emerged from research by Howard (2001) into plagiarism. Plagiarism is considered to be the passing off of work done by someone else, intentionally or unintentionally, as your own, for your own benefit (Carroll, 2002). The difficulty with plagiarism is that there are degrees of plagiarism and this, to some extent, overlaps with collusion and cheating. What is important to understand about plagiarism is that the passing off of work by someone else is related to giving a false impression, or of fooling or tricking. While this could be seen to be deliberate dishonesty, plagiarism is also difficult territory because whether the tricking was intentional or unintentional, it is still classed as plagiarism. While there has been a focus, in the UK at least, on catching the guilty and creating software to make sure no ones gets away with anything, such a heavy-handed approach assumes guilt and does little to explore the underlying difficulties students are encountering. For example, although difference in cultural practices and not understanding what counts as plagiarism are seen as the central reasons for plagiarism, the innovative work of Howard (2001) and the study by Pecorari (2003) shed new light on this troublesome area. Howard (2001) suggests that new writers rely on the language of the source materials that they utilize, something she terms 'patchwriting'. Thus, what she is suggesting is that patchwriting is an essential phase through which writers progress as their voices emerge. A more recent study (Pecorari, 2003) explored plagiarism with postgraduate students in order to examine the possibilities for, and prevalence of, patchwriting. Pecorari found: 'Patchwriting, then, differs from plagiarism ... in two ways: It lacks the element of intentional deception, and it is not a terminal stage. Today's patchwriter is tomorrow's competent academic writer, given the necessary support to develop' (Pecorari, 2003: 338).

What is particularly important about this work is the recognition that patchwriting is not only a widespread strategy, but also that it is a process through which students, and possibility academics, pass as they develop a writer identity and voice. Thus patchwriting is not only something that bears further research but also needs to be properly acknowledged, so that writers can be helped to move away from patched identities in ways that help to develop a writer voice. Patched identities may also be seen in expert seminars, conference presentations and keynote speeches. Here the authors (speakers) appear voiceless and rely heavily on the work of others. This form of patched identity seems to emerge due to a lack of the sense of the authors believing they have a strong or unique stance on the subject, a position from which to speak, and thus they rely on other voices to patch some perspectives together.

Representative identities

It could be argued, and increasingly is, that cyberspace has resulted in a sense of multiple identities and disembodiment, or even different forms of embodiment. Further, the *sense* of anonymity and the assumption that this was what was understood through one's words rather than one's bodily presence, is becoming increasingly unmasked through virtual worlds such as Second Life. The bodily markers that are used to present ourselves in life – clothes, ethnicity, gender and speech – may be re-presented (differently) in Second Life, but they also indicate choices about how we wish to be seen or the ways in which we might like to feel differently. Furthermore, authors such as Seymour (2001) have suggested that although the physical body is invisible, meanings, mannerisms, behaviours and unstated assumptions are clearly visible in online communication.

Yet in the process of trying out new identities in a virtual world, what I would term our representative identities, questions arise about the impact of these representative identities on our physical, embodied or place-based identities. For example, to what extent do virtual world identities spill over into work or home identities and impact on or prompt reformulations of other identities in other 'worlds?' Further, how do we represent ourselves differently in face-to-face worlds? For example, Malcolm and Zukas (2005) discuss the meanings attached to 'real hours' in academic life in the context of workload management. They argue that not only do 'real hours' differ across disciplines but also that academic work is not bounded by the office and department. Thus, the way in which our identities are represented across home, work and disciplines differ. This is exemplified in a reflection about the description of the preparation of their conference paper:

> Everyone at this conference knows that it is not bounded by the office, the department, or the university. This paper was developed and partly written at a kitchen table in London – some way away from either of our offices or homes; one of us usually does her marking in bed; some of our best ideas originate whilst performing ablutions; conference presentations are often developed in hotel rooms and research programmes written at motorway cafes. Despite this, even in these times of flexible and distributed work and learning, the 'official version' of institutional practices and discourses operates as if the academic workplace were fixed and static. (Malcolm and Zukas, 2005)

We choose to represent ourselves as not working in bed or marking at the kitchen table, and yet many of us do exactly that.

There is a further interesting juxtaposition of real life (RL) and Second Life (SL), and the extent to which one feels more 'real' in SL than in online discussions. There seems to be something about being able to represent oneself visually, being able to make choices about what one looks like and how one can move, that gives a stronger sense of *being* present even if one is not. Perhaps this is related to being able to *choose* how to represent oneself or to do with feeling *more embodied*. What is also important in the whole issue of virtual worlds such as Second Life is

- The pedagogy of such worlds
- The pedagogical possibilities underlying these worlds.

For example, it might be that virtual worlds and gaming not only have different, or diverse, underlying pedagogies (and pedagogical possibilities), but also the assumptions that are made about issues of power and control in games where avatars are representative of 'someone else'; as opposed to a representation of one's own identities.

However, there remain questions to be answered about the extent to which identity shifts, as well as role shifts, are more likely to occur in some environments than others. Perhaps Gee's work on video gaming offers some sense not only of the multiplicity of identities involved in online learning, but also the possibilities for relationships between some of them. One of the difficulties related to games-based learning would seem to be that of identity. Gee (2004: 112–13) developed a theory of identity, based on experience of videogaming. It is a tripartite identity comprising:

1. The real identity: who we are in the physical world
2. The virtual identity: who we are in the virtual space. Thus, Gee argues, our virtual self should be able to 'inherit' some of our real attributes
3. The projected identity: the projected identity refers to identity that is developed through engaging with the character, through the interaction of the first two identities.

However, Gee's conception of the virtual self here is located in gaming and the character within the games, and his notion of identity here seems to equate with 'role' rather than identity *per se*. Further, he has argued that identities are projected identities, but this introduces interesting psycho-analytic difficulties. Projections are usually unwanted feelings that we invari-ably choose not to own. We therefore believe that someone else is thinking/feeling them instead, such as anger or judgement (see, for example, Jung, 1977). Avatars in Second Life seem, in general, to capture wanted elements, or the chosen components of our identities that we wish to present to/in the world. Thus in virtual worlds it would seem that the identities presented are more likely to be the functional or ideal sides rather than the projected 'unwanted' sides.

In the more recent virtual worlds, such as Second Life, identities are not limited to games or to one's individual character in a game. The wide range of choices available in Second Life, in terms of the creation of an avatar, often confound participants. The confusions emerge through choices of representation, for example, whether to ensure the avatar looks 'more like us', since this may create a great sense of comfort and decrease dis-ease or not, since it forces us to confront how we see ourselves and how we want others to see us. However, the location of one's avatar in spaces such as Second Life poses particular complexities, because of the interaction of five interrelated concerns that play out in the 'social space.' These are:

• The 'real' body, in the sense of the interlocutor of the avatar, the 'author'
• The choice of physical representation and the way the avatar is presented to others
• The relationship between the avatar and the author
• The author's lived experience and the social representations made through the avatar
• The intentional meanings represented through the avatar.

The assumption that follows is that there is a world out there (the real) that can be captured by a 'knowing' author through the careful transcription of one's roles into the avatar. Yet both in research and in Second Life it would seem that language and speech are not representations that mirror experience, but instead create it, thus the meanings ascribed and inscribed in and through avatars are always on the move. It might be that liminality could be seen as a trope for understanding avatar identity/pedagogy, or possibly that provisionality and representation might be seen as subcategories of liminality itself. Yet it is probably more likely that provisionality and representation are issues that inform our understandings of liminality. For example, struggles with understandings of what might constitute provisionality and how representation affects avatar identity and avatar pedagogy can inform and guide the different forms and formulations of liminality that occur in three-dimensional (3D) worlds. Yet the issues of provisionality and representation and their relationship with liminality introduces questions about whether liminality differs in real life compared with 3D virtual worlds and whether different forms of liminality exist and/or can be delineated. For example, is the liminality that emerges because of learning in a 3D world different from the liminality that occurs in face-to-face learning? Is it that the liminality prompted/provoked by 3D worlds is a more lonely experience because it is less usual and possibly less ordered?

Furthermore, there has been relatively little consideration of agency in 3D worlds and author/avatar as the primary informing relation/opposition. Yet agency in-world is devolved in very novel ways, such as particular activities or functions that can be scripted to make avatars respond in particular ways, which challenge us to extend the simple author/avatar relation to a broader consideration of agency as it is reconstituted by the multiple relations between author/avatar/world. Thus Gee's descriptions of different formulations of identity would seem to deny the possibility for constant identity transition and transformation, whether through the impact of the author on the avatar or vice versa.

Provisional identities

The notion of provisional identities captures the idea that our identities are constantly changing and thus we are always necessarily on the move. Further, our identities do not always sit easily with one another, therefore collision and uncertainty result in disquietude and a sense of fragmentation. However, Land et al. would argue against such identity positions, arguing for the need for provisional stabilities:

> the process of acquiring new knowledge tends to involve what Bonamy *et al* (2001) would call 'provisional stabilities', this means that over the course of an entire programme such periods of letting-go and reconstitution will be repeated and call for metacognitive skills on the part of the learner to cope with such transformation and to tolerate uncertainty. (Land et al., 2005: 64)

Yet this degree of stability is something that shifts in time, space and place. Thus rather than locating provisional stability as soothing, related to the condition of 'normless' (Durkheim, 1952) that seems to occur in rapid periods of change, perhaps it is better to locate the idea away from a notion of possible or provisional stability. Instead, it is argued here that the global learners of the twenty-first century – whether staff or students – largely live and work in a position of *chronic uncertainty.* In terms of rapid policy change in higher education, perhaps chronic uncertainty might be the most effective way in which to operate! The result of such a position of uncertainty would not be a position of provisional stability but one of provisional identity construction. Although the work of Durkheim would suggest that such chronic uncertainty is a threat to society, there are those, such as Beck, who might argue that chronic uncertainty is reflected though a risk society. Reflexive modernization, the process by which the classical industrial society has modernized itself, has resulted in a sense of crisis characterized by a 'risk society' (Beck, 1992). This type of society, with its emerging themes of ecological safety, the danger of losing control over scientific and technological innovations and the growth of a more flexible labour force, has and continues to have a profound effect on higher education. For example, the university now increasingly guards against what might fail within the system, such as ethical standards, plagiarism, economic viability and student failure. The result is, I would suggest, a focus not just on quality assurance but quality *insurance.*

Yet, perhaps part of the issue here is that in learning there is little room for stability, since knowledge and learning always appear to be on the move. Thus, it is questionable as to whether one can have any kind of stability in uncertain stuck spaces. Such stuck spaces are not only transient spaces but also spaces where it is possible to see that what one once believed to be truths and ways of being are now merely contingent and provisional. Thus by living with/in provisional identities means expecting that resilience and constant renewal is to be a life companion. Therefore possible ways of living with provisional identities, in a state of chronic uncertainty means any combination of the following six headings:

Embracing dilemmas

There is a tendency in higher education, globally, to either ignore dilemmas, to attempt to resolve them quickly or to rationalize the situation, often blaming someone else for the difficulty. Yet to sit with these dilemmas often results in greater self-understanding and a means of moving forward which may not initially have presented itself. O'Reilly (1989) has argued that there are risks involved in moving from experience that is incoherent to making public statements about one's self. For example, experience is often incoherent and in speaking of experience to others (publicly) is to risk sounding as if our experience is meaningless, contradictory and multiple (which it probably is).

Learning to live with tensions and moving between tensions iteratively

To embrace dilemmas means also to live not only with tensions, but sometimes in a constant state of tension. To move between possibilities offers the opportunity to be open to new ways of thinking, of engaging with different and diverse forms of information and of considering different personal and pedagogical stances.

Living with open boundaries

To live with open boundaries is to assume, always, that life and learning is unfinished, unresolved, irresolvable and unknowable. Open boundaries are therefore necessarily problematic but engaging with them results in continuous identity modification becoming a state of being.

Valuing doubt

While doubt is something that is usually seen as negative, here it is suggested that doubt is a means of moving away from a liminal space. Instead of trying to eliminate doubt in learning and in knowledge creation, it is better to realize it and value it so that both staff and students see doubt and uncertainty as central principles of learning.

Acknowledging the importance of third spaces

The notion of the 'third space' captures the idea that there are 'particular discursive spaces . . . in which alternative and competing discourses and positioning transform conflict and difference into rich zones of collaboration and learning.' (Gutiérrez et al., 1999: 286–7). These spaces tend to be polycontextual, multivoiced and multiscripted. Although the research by Gutiérrez et al. relates to children learning across languages and cultures, the notion of third spaces is helpful in locating and understanding the languages, discourses and cultures implicit within disciplinary pedagogies. By enabling students and new staff to comprehend and negotiate a third space it can help them move away from a liminal space. Such negotiation will involve engaging with official and unofficial spaces, allowing parallels to be drawn between hybrid genres, knowledges, humour and official and unofficial worlds.

Recognising limits

By recognizing the limit of our language capabilities and our language we can begin to see limits as paths towards something which are necessarily also away from something else. Therefore learning to live with limits helps us to see that ways away from provisional identities also bring other limits, not only the recognition of our own limits but also the limits of cultures, gender and society that require us to acknowledge 'conscientization' (Freire, 1974). This is the process whereby people come to understand that both their views of the world and their situation within it are shaped by social and historical forces that can work against their own interests. Thus by recognizing limits and in order to effect change it is vital that we live in a constant state of conscientization.

However, perhaps what is also important about living with provisional identities is the development of greater self-understanding, a sense of understanding our own stories better and 'in relation' to other stories, theories and texts. Thus, ways of managing provisional identities must address ways of enabling people to create maps and make meanings and connections for themselves.

Conclusion

Spatial identities are identities on the move, shaped by changing practices and cultures in higher education. Despite the increasing materialization of the risk society and attempts to manage 'the bad', it would seem that there is an emergence of further uncertainty and different kinds of risk. Such risk can be seen in the locale of spatial identities where Web 2.0 technologies have reduced possibilities for all kinds of control. Blogs and wikis have promoted the framing and reconstitution of textual identities, although it might be argued that these have become increasingly egocentric and confessional in nature. Moreover, digital game-based learning and virtual worlds continue to challenge academics to consider the interaction of play and learning. The result is a society not only characterized by uncertainty and ambiguity, but also by liminal spaces and identities. The university needs to consider how to respond to such a position and how to stand for/against the challenges that emerge from these new spatial zones and practices.

10

Re-positioning Learning Spaces

The final chapter of this volume argues that if the university is to maintain some leverage in the world of intellectual thought, then it needs to regain learning spaces as places in which in-depth deliberation and intellectual positioning can occur. This chapter delineates ways of repositioning curricula to equip staff and students to live and work in an uncertain world. In particular it outlines possibilities for reviewing the university as a space and suggests that, with the increasing presence of chronic uncertainty, perhaps liminal curricula and universities may offer a possible way forward.

University as place and space

It would seem that higher education has increasingly become colonized by an enterprise culture and the result is that academics have become defined by and through this culture. There is also an economic issue here in the sense that in the context of new managerialism the university is seen as an efficient producer of skilled workers but such a position prevents the acknowledgement or recognition of the need for space and thus all 'slack hours' are removed. The colonizers of higher education have therefore been seeking to change academic identities and practices in the ways that reflect those of the colonizers. The consequence is that academic voices are becoming divided across different cultures and languages. Many academics feel displaced and divorced from their previous habitats and dislocated within the new and imposed ones. These colonizing forms of enterprise in higher education reflect the market forces and the quick fix stance of commerce and industry. Higher education that only supplies 'training' is unlikely to equip students to work in an uncertain world.

Yet perhaps a collegial model of higher education, with its emphasis on freedom, disciplinarity and the student as knowledge apprentice is also unhelpful. Barnett (2003) has argued that universities are positioning and repositioning themselves willy-nilly, with the result that there is no longer a

sense of their purpose. Yet it is not entirely clear from Barnett's argument how this repositioning might be located and mapped in ways that
facilitate the delineation of new learning spaces and places for curriculum
reinvention. Instead he suggests that as a result of the chaos, universities are
becoming sites of ideology both from external forces but perhaps more per-
niciously from within. Thus he argues for two forms of ideology: virtuous,
such as disciplinarity and professional development, and pernicious which
includes issues such as quality and entrepreneurship. The hope he suggests
is in idealogies, which are ideologies that are deliberately constructed around
the ideals and perceptions the university has of itself. Yet in many universities
it would seem that such ideals and perceptions are diverse and often
unmanageable; so that Barnett's stance would seem too optimistic.

Yet what is particularly helpful is his notion of ideological spaces, a space in
which academics might take up a stance towards the dominant ideologies of
the institution. The ideals of a university are surely seen then in the future
professionals who are being developed through it and the ways in which
different universities and different disciplines prepare students for different
kinds of uncertainties. Perhaps mapping universities across ideologies, idealogies and typologies might offer a clearer sense of the landscape. Furthermore, deconstructing fashionable ideas and practices in higher education
can help us to understand the way in which it is used as a particular form
of social production. For example, the continuing focus on competence to
practice in many professional curricula has downgraded the value of thinking, reasoning and the position of criticality within the curriculum. The
result, as Fuller (2006) has argued, is that the university is destroying social
capital. Further, particular higher education practices are used to control
and maintain power structures and relationships in universities, whether it is
the male-dominated professorial selection board or the female-guided teaching and learning committee. At the same time there seem to be shifts away
from arguments that higher education reflects postmodernity. Certainly it
would seem that Barnett's more recent works (for example, 2003; 2004)
reflect a location in late modernity, while Burbules is suspicious of the cat-
egory of 'postmodernity' partly because it is used to represent a wide variety
of authors and approaches but also because he believes that the relationship
between postmodernity and modernity is misunderstood. He argues (like
Giddens, 1991) that postmodernism is a product of modernity, not a surpass-
ing of it. Perhaps our hope should be in incredulity towards metanarratives
such as Lyotard (1979) suggested, so that constant incredulity will continually result in challenges towards performative notions of truth, rules and
regulations and 'knowledge to go' (Perkins, 2006a).

Rethinking the university as space

Universities continue to be seen as having stable identities which are relatively apolitical and which are places of educating students for life, but more

particularly, these days, for the world of work. Yet they are increasingly being destabilized not only by external expectations of governments, but more so by the changing nature of students and the impact of unruly and destabilizing technologies. Universities are also likely to be destabilized by the shifting terrain within new spaces such as Second Life, whereby creating business and selling products are changing notions of work-related learning, learning, spatial learning practices, conceptions of teaching and the relationship between play, games and learning. The notion of *learning architecture* is useful here since it helps to create different understandings of learning: learning as an architectured space, such as a beach in Second Life, or the way that teaching and learning are architected to create particular practices and performances by students. Learning architecture might encompass the following learning spaces.

Pedagogy and play

The increasing need to manage the interplay of identities in face-to-face lives is further complicated by managing the embodied identities of the virtual world. For example, working and learning in virtual worlds, such as Second Life, introduces juxtaposition and crossover between real life and Second Life where we take our multiple pasts with us. This would seem to suggest that we are in late modernity and that as we are travelling into/in/with Web 2.0 technologies, we need a university that engages more thoroughly with these third spaces. Such a university would enable an exploration of the ways in which past, current and future identities are present and embodied and multiply interacting with each other in these spaces. Further, there are issues about learning, play and fun and how we also play in and through our identities in virtual spaces. Rieber et al. (1998) have suggested that the notion of 'serious play', which is characterized as an intense learning experience, involves considerable energy and commitment. The author suggests that serious play is important for the development of high-order thinking, commitment and engagement. Second Life identities are those that would seem to be *at play* in this way, it is a demanding and engaging environment, whether travelling and exploring, or participating in seminars. Universities of the future will need to develop spaces in worlds such as this, but also utilize games and play effectively – whether through game playing or games design.

However, there are those who argue not for play *per se*, but for playing with the rules:

> Knowledge is created through disciplinary tensions in particular institutional settings . . . it makes little sense to apologise for the institutionality of academics' thought when institutionality makes it academicism. What one can do however is play with the disciplinary rules and boundaries. There are always techniques for managing the university that alter the forms of knowledge produced; there are always marginalised knowledges

that can unsettle complacent conventions of the centre. (Game and Metcalf, 1996: 25)

Yet this kind of quiet subversion is not enough. Playing with the rules will not help to re-create, to reposition learning spaces. What is required is not just playing with the boundaries but shifting them, moving them, transcending them. Curricula need to be seen not just as content for meddling with, but as diverse spaces of opportunity. It is in such spaces that we can explore the possibilities for creating curricula for chronic uncertainty, liminality and spaces of unknowability. Curricula then will become a series of open-ended spaces rather than a series of permissions to proceed that focus on compliance and rule-based models. Such open-ended curricula will be provisional, unstable and uncertain, and will reflect the translocational state of the university of the future.

Being an academic nomad

The notion of being an academic nomad reflects the sense that being an academic in higher education is about the development of one's identity through knowledge reconstruction, creation and understanding, it is about self-emancipation. As Fuller (2006) has argued, the university is the site for the manufacture of knowledge for the public good and making knowledge(s) that the public demand is (are) taught, explored, explained and meddled with. Teaching is not merely about asking students to gain knowledge, but to engage with diverse forms of knowledge for their enlightenment. As Fuller has suggested, liberal education, certainly in the UK, is not given its due. The result is that gaining a degree is more about marginal advantage in the job market than about personal transformation. Yet academics should be creating curricula and engaging with forms of knowledge that create disturbance both for themselves and their students.

However, recent studies (such as Cooper, 2006) have indicated that the notion of 'being' a teacher in higher education continues to be a problematic and contested space. While at first glance it might seem to be because of divisions between research and teaching roles and the growth of the portfolio academic, it is more complex than this. The emphasis on postgraduate certificates in teaching for staff and the global interest in the scholarship of teaching and learning, along with the rivers of money provided to develop Centres for Excellence in Teaching and Learning in the UK, has resulted in some interesting conundrums. Staff are becoming aware of discipline-based pedagogies and the impact of this on the constructions of pedagogical signatures. The creation of dialogic spaces about teaching for academics has resulted in a realization of the lack of support at a middle management level for such spaces, and for some academics the notion of being a learner while being a lecturer is deeply problematic both emotionally and pedagogically. Thus, the emphasis on the scholarship of learning and teaching has created disjunctive spaces, spaces of conflict and contestation where identity construction is problematic.

Re-engaging with chance and contingency

Instead of repudiating chronic uncertainty, the university needs to live with contingency and discomfort. Lack of understanding about power, management decisions and decision-making in universities appears to hide powerful spatial practices. This is because much of the decision-making is made away from the gaze of most academics who are informed of resolutions through newsletters and email. For example, Soja has argued: 'We must be insistently aware of how space can be made to hide consequences from us, how relations of power and discipline are inscribed into the apparently innocent spatiality of social life, how human geographies become filled with politics and ideology' (Soja, 1989: 6) Thus, as Soja suggests, the importance of space is hidden by two forms of opacity, an empiricist focus on immediate appearances and an illusion of transparency.

The university should be situationally created, and learning and teaching need to be rethought (again) as a position of co-construction. Therefore the continual need to close loops at all levels of the university must stop. In practice this will mean not just an uncertain university but also a liminal one. Closing loops results in closed systems and practices and prevents the migration of uncertainty in decision-making and curricula spaces.

Re-architecturing learning spaces

The question now is how the university begins to engage with third spaces, engages with liminal identities and moves away from performativity. To argue for such a position could be seen as a lone voice in a silent space, yet there is a proliferation of stances emerging (for example Bayne, 2005a, 2005b; McWilliam, 2005; Nixon, 2005; Haggis, 2006; Land, 2006; Manathunga, 2006). Such voices are vital for reconceptualizing and recasting what it means to be a university, but the difficulty remains as to how any of the ideas, ideologies and arguments are to be acted upon. Some might argue that introducing more problem-based learning or different formulations of work-based learning are enough. However, what we seem to require is a new constellation of learning spaces, a revitalized sense of what it means to be a university. Perhaps the question is what might a third space university look like and how might it practice? Certainly Barnett's perspective on super-complexity and the suggestions of the development of curricula that equip students for an unknowable world is a useful pointer (Barnett, 2000). Yet his work is reflective of the early 2000s, and what is required now is a different place to stand. It might be that what is needed instead is an uncertain university where contingency and liminality are the organizing principles of the curriculum. Alternatively, it might be that different typologies of university are required, focusing on different kinds of learning spaces and provision. However, third space or liminal universities would be the kinds of learning spaces which engage with the following concerns. For example, it is possible to locate curriculum types not only through the way learning is seen and structured, but also through the way in which modes of knowledge are located in the curriculum. By seeing curricula anew as learning spaces it may be possible to offer curricula that shift beyond performativity and are liminal in nature. Thus it may be possible to see curricula as striated, borderland, smooth or troublesome. Inevitably, the distinction and the boundaries between these models collide and overlap, but perhaps they might offer different ways of seeing and structuring curricula, and help us to move away from outcome-based models.

Striated curricula

It appears that apart from the kind of education that occurs in the liberal arts colleges of the USA, most curricula worldwide are striated. These curricula are characterized by a strong sense of organization and boundedness. Thus learning in such spaces is epitomized through course attendance, defined learning places such as lecture theatres and classrooms, and with the use of (often set) books. Further, these spaces are bounded not only through the traditions of the discipline and the signature pedagogies, but also by university structures and procedures. Such striated systems mean that learning spaces are diminished, and personal engagement with such spaces is often demeaned by others. Dialogue, writing and reflection are not only undervalued, but also viewed with quiet contempt, as being privileged, utopian spaces.

Borderland curricula

These curricula sit at the boundaries of smooth and striated spaces. There are characteristics of striation present in terms of the way curricula are organized, but the control possibilities for open-endedness are visible. Learning in these spaces promotes the use of critical thought to decentre identities from disciplines in order to transcend them. Staff may transcend boundaries but they are unlikely to challenge the frameworks into which disciplinary knowledge is placed. In the border spaces decentring involves reflection upon, and an openness towards, the stances of others and therefore necessarily an evaluation of one's own. It is also about integrating what one knows tacitly with what else is on offer and as a result integrating and transcending boundaries simultaneously, whether smooth or striated. Thus there is not only a sense of the transdisciplinary in these spaces but opportunities for contesting what counts as curriculum. The difficulty in these curricula spaces is that the smoothness is often hidden by the striated practices of the university. Therefore negotiation and playing at the borders are evident here but they may be less obvious than in smooth curricula because of being hidden behind other structures.

Smooth curricula

Smooth curricula spaces are open, flexible and contested, spaces in which both learning and learners are always on the move. Movement in such curricula is not towards a given trajectory; instead, there is a sense of displacement of notions of time and place, so that curricula are delineated with and through the staff and students – they are defined by the creators of the space(s). These kinds of curricula are likely to be seen as risky since they prompt consideration of what counts as legitimate knowledge. In these kinds of curricula students will be encouraged to examine the underlying structures and belief systems implicit within what is being learned, in order to not only understand the disciplinary area but also its credence. What will be important in the creation of these kinds of curricula is the position of disregarded knowledge as a central space, in which uncertainty and gaps are recognized along with the realization of the relative importance of gaps between different knowledge and different knowledge hierarchies.

Troublesome curricula

These curricula are characterized by learning opportunities that prompt engagement with disjunction. While it is argued here that designing liminality into a curriculum is not a possibility since liminal experiences are largely related to identity shifts, designing spaces that allow disjunction to occur can prompt shifts towards liminality. Thus in such curricula suspended states that may occur within it can serve as a transformative function, as someone moves from one state or position to another. In these curricula proactive learning would be central, since the expectation would be that one would acquire a new stance, a different vision, an active leap away from previous perspectives, both as teacher and learner. The use of messy problems and collaborative learning can be a useful means of designing troublesome curricula, but what is important here is to see curricula being characterized by perpetual liminality and chronic uncertainty, which are promoted through disjunction and troublesome knowledge. Thus it might be possible to delineate these modes, somewhat crudely, as in Table 10.1.

Yet we are left at the end with some questions about what might constitute a university that has or is in the process of recreating learning spaces:

1. What are the kinds of identities a liminal university might produce/ promote?

Table 10.1 Curricula for an uncertain world

Curriculum position	Striated	Borderland	Smooth	Troublesome
Curriculum focus	Outcomes and organization	Boundary transcendence	Space creation	Disjunction and uncertainty
Mode of knowledge	Modes 1 and 2	Mode 2 and 3	Mode 4	Modes 3 to 5
Types of learning	Solid learning	Lumpy learning	Liquid learning	Liquid learning
Conceptions of knowing	Retention and application	Finding connections	Gap realization	Active adventuring
Types of prompts to learning	Routine preparation and rehearsal	Deconstructing structures	Invitation to discover	Messy dilemmas
Position of student	Inert	Finding connections	Locating gaps	Actively alert

2. What kinds of spaces might construct identities for a late modern and supercomplex world?
3. How is learning for this world to be negotiated, constructed and embodied as a social practice?

Re-positioning learning spaces?

Universities are still attempting to ensure that they are password-protected enclosures and most remain resistant to new spatial practices. For students who spend over six hours a day on social networking and just over three hours a day on email, surfing the net and instant messaging (Harris Interactive, 2006), it is clear universities need to rethink digital learning spaces. Space, such as Facebook and MySpace, can tell us much about what interests and motivates students and can begin to offer us some ideas about how to change learning spaces for students and academics. While some subscribe to Prensky's (2001) notion of digital natives, the idea that students who are born into the digital world are native speakers of the language of computers, video games and the Internet, it is too simplistic an idea. This is because those people who were already born when the Internet 'arrived' are natives too, in the sense that they were established and grew with the changes and adapted accordingly. Furthermore, there are many academics who are as familiar with Web 2.0 spaces as students, and are just as excited about its possibilities. Thus, it is important to note that many academics are frustrated with many of the constraints of Web 1.0 facilities in their universities. Web 2.0 offers a different textuality, since they are rewritable technologies that are increasingly ushering in new issues and concerns, such as consensus over authority and process over product. Indeed, what also seems to be emerging from Web 2.0 spaces is not just a different textuality, but the spatialization of knowledge, whereby knowledge is multiply located and linked, reconstituted and contested across time and space. For example, Flickr and del.icio.us are not only social networks, but are increasingly changing the nature of open source ware and the notions of knowledge and knowledge ownership. Furthermore, in virtual worlds and even game spaces temporality and spatiality become not just contested but dynamic and intersected by one another. Such spaces exist, yet do not exist, they are bounded but provisional.

Perhaps what is needed is to create not universities but ruins, to create borderless spaces, much as the University of Bologna once was. To strip universities of their architectured and disciplinary walls will interrupt established practice and the power inherent in those practices. Giroux and Giroux have argued that educators should build courses by combining 'democratic principles, values, and practices with . . . the histories and struggles of those often marginalized because of race, class, gender, disability, or age' (2004: 99). They argue that academics should shift beyond the lands of academia and integrate with the larger spheres in the community, where culture and politics are truly learned and made relevant. Thus if we continue to engage with performative enterprise practices and fail to re-create spaces and voices, universities will soon become sites of closure, where criticality and questioning are submerged in the quest for fast money and solid learning. Thus universities need to rethink their interpretive repertoire (Potter and Wetherall, 1987), since much of higher education still locates itself with the values about how teaching and research should operate. Certainly at higher management levels of universities the concerns are more related to how large sums of money might be gained to sustain the university, rather than the nature or value of teaching. Yet students are engaged in forms of social learning and networking that transgress these spaces and values. What needs to be done is the reconstitution of what learning and teaching *might be*, what a university *might be for* in an uncertain world. Thus as argued for above, the university needs to develop hybrid identities, to decamp from its current spaces and camp in the border spaces.

Perhaps what we should be aiming for is a vision for a troublesome university, where liquid learning and Web 2.0 or even Web 3.0 spaces become the dominant spaces of engagement. Yet a troublesome university would need to stretch beyond open source ware and closed virtual environments. Instead, it would need to be created around a constellation of uncertainties such as smooth or liminal curricula, negotiated assessment, mobile learning and rewritable learning intentions. Thus the credentializing degree of the university will become where voice and argument of both staff and students are centre stage and universities become re-created as spaces of enlightenment.

Conclusion

The university to some extent remains a partitioned-off space where policy and expectations of governments are increasingly seen as given rather than negotiable, contingent or contextual, both in terms of space, place and discipline. The space of the university has not only been affected by policy change related to funding for improving teaching and developing research, but it has also been reframed through imposed activities related to quality and research agenda. What also arrives with such imposed activities are the metaphors to sustain them and the positions adopted by those who support them. However, seeing the university as a site for reclaiming the lost, the new or the marginalized learning spaces, offers opportunities to stand against the current practices that mitigate against the possibility of such reclamation. Such a vision however, will require that we stop seeing the university as a predictable, ordered and manageable space, but instead re-view it as an important site of transformation characterized by risk, uncertainty and radical unknowability.

Glossary

Avatar   The bodily manifestation of one's self in the context of a three-dimensional virtual world.

Aporia (Greek: ἀπορία *impasse*; *lack of resources; puzzlement; embarrassment*)   A puzzle or an impasse, but it can also denote the state of being perplexed, or at a loss, at such a puzzle or impasse.

Blogs (weblogs)   Personal websites consisting of regularly updated entries displayed in reverse chronological order. They may be used by learners in PBLonline to evidence their thinking openly to the rest of the team and the e-tutor.

Boundary spaces   Spaces within civic society, which are in-between spaces, spaces between cultures and politics, between people and institutions and between diverse forms of knowledges.

Commodification   The turning of an object into a commodity, where it has some exchange value, other than the effort taken in its production. With the wider reader audience offered by technology, students find a value for their writing that goes beyond the grade.

Community of practice   A group of professionals informally bound to one another through exposure to common problems and common pursuit of solutions thereby generating within themselves a body of 'expert' knowledge.

Constructionism   This learning philosophy states that learning is best when the learner is engaged in an active role of designer and constructor, especially where the learner is consciously engaged in constructing something that will be shared, for example, with other members of a virtual team (see Papert, 1986).

Constructivism   This learning theory is based on the concept that knowledge is created by the learner based on mental activity. Conceptual growth comes from sharing individual constructions and changing perceptions in response to the perceptions of others. Learning is best situated in an environment reflective of real world contexts (Piaget, 1928).

Critical contestability   A position whereby students understand and acknowledge the transient nature of subject and discipline boundaries. They are able to transcend and interrogate these boundaries through a commitment to exploring the subtext of subjects and disciplines.

Cyberspace   Currently used to describe the whole range of information resources available through computer networks.

Dialogic learning Learning that occurs when insights and understandings emerge through dialogue in a learning environment. It is a form of learning where students draw upon their own experience to explain the concepts and ideas with which they are presented, and then use that experience to make sense for themselves and also to explore further issues.

Dialogic spaces Spaces that transcend conceptions of dialogue, which are invariably conceived as the notions of exchange of ideas, and dialectic as the conception of transformation through contestability. Dialogic spaces also encompass the complex relationship that occurs between oral and written communication and the way, in particular, that written communication is understood by the reader.

Digital spaces Those spaces in which communication and interaction are assisted, created or enhanced by digital media.

Disjunction A sense of fragmentation of part of, or all of the self, characterized by frustration and confusion, and a loss of sense of self, which often results in anger and the need for right answers.

Domain The overlapping spheres within each stance. The borders of the domains merge with one another and therefore shifts between domains are transitional areas where particular kinds of learning occur.

Electracy The creation of pedagogies that will enable the integration of Internet practices with literate skills in new and innovative ways.

Interactional stance The ways in which learners work and learn in groups and construct meaning in relation to one another.

Learner identity An identity formulated through the interaction of learner and learning. The notion of learner identity moves beyond, but encapsulates the notion of learning style, and encompasses positions that students take up in learning situations, whether consciously or unconsciously.

Learning bridges Mechanisms that help to link or connect different past and present positions in ways that enable shifts to be made – whether transitional or transformative.

Learning context The interplay of all the values, beliefs, relationships, frameworks and external structures that operate within a given learning environment.

Learning stances The three stances (personal, pedagogical and interactional) that together form the framework of dimensions of learner experience.

Liminality Characterized by a stripping away of old identities and an oscillation between states, it is a betwixt and between state and there is a sense of being in a period of transition, often on the way to a new or different space.

Liquid learning Characterised by emancipation, reflexivity and flexibility so that knowledge and knowledge boundaries are contestable and always on the move.

Lurking A person who reads chatroom discussions, group or message board postings, but does not contribute.

Managed learning environment (MLE) A software system designed to assist teachers in managing online educational programmes. It includes access control, e-learning content, communication tools and the administration of user groups.

Mode 1 knowledge (Gibbons et al., 1994) Propositional knowledge that is produced within the academe separate from its use. The academe is considered the traditional environment for the generation of Mode 1 knowledge.

Mode 2 knowledge (Gibbons et al., 1994) Knowledge that transcends disciplines and is produced in, and validated through the world of work. Knowing in this mode demands the integration of skills and abilities in order to act in a particular context.

Net generation The generation that has barely known a world without computers, the World Wide Web, highly interactive video games and mobile phones. For many of this generation instant messaging, rather than telephone or email, is the primary form of communication.

Pedagogical stance   The ways in which people see themselves as learners in particular educational environments.

Performativity   The increasing focus in higher education on what students are able to *do*, which has emerged from the desire to equip students for life and work. Higher education is sliding towards encouraging students to perform rather than to necessarily critique and do.

Personal stance   The way in which staff and students see themselves in relation to the learning context and give their own distinctive meaning to their experience of that context.

Posting (verb)   To publish a message on an online forum or discussion group.

Posting (noun)   A message published on an online forum or discussion group.

Problem-based learning   An approach to learning where the focus for learning is problem situations, rather than content. Students work in small teams and are facilitated by a tutor.

Problem-based learning online   A generic term which captures that vast variety of ways in which problem-based learning is being used synchronously and asynchronously, on campus, or at a distance. It represents the idea that students learn through web-based materials including text, simulations, videos and demonstrations, and resources such as chatrooms, message boards and environments that have been purpose-built for problem-based learning.

Problem-based learning team   A number of students (eight to ten) who work together as a defined group.

Problem-solving learning   Teaching where the focus is on students solving a given problem by acquiring the answers expected by the lecturer, answers that are rooted in the information supplied in some way to the students. The solutions are bounded by the content and students are expected to explore little extra material other than that with which they have been provided, in order to discover the solutions.

Reflective spaces   Spaces in which our constructions of reality are no longer reinforced by the forces of our sociocultural world, so that we begin to move from a state or position of reflection into reflective spaces.

Scaffolding   The concept of scaffolding is based on Vygotsky's zone of proximal development. Individualized support designed to facilitate a student's ability to build on prior knowledge and to generate and internalize new knowledge is provided by the tutor or other students. The support is pitched just beyond the current level of the student.

Screenager: Member of a younger generation of students who have found, through their engagement with new digital technologies, a means of thriving in environments of uncertainty and complexity.

Second Life   A three-dimensional virtual world created by LindenLab set in an Internet-based world. Residents (in the forms of self-designed avatars) in this world interact with each other and can learn, socialize, participate in activities, and buy and sell items with one another

Smooth spaces   Open, flexible and contested spaces in which both learning and learners are always on the move. Students here would be encouraged to contest knowledge and ideas proffered by the lecturers and in doing so create their own stance towards knowledge(s).

Spatial ecology   The creation of balance between and across spaces in higher education, so that account is taken of not merely knowledge, content, conceptions and acquisition but also of ontology, values and beliefs, uncertainty and complexity.

Stance   One's attitude, belief or disposition towards a particular context, person or experience. It refers to a particular position one takes up in life towards something, at a particular point in time.

Striated spaces   Spaces characterized by a strong sense of organization and boundedness. Learning in such spaces is epitomized through course attendance, and defined learning places such as lecture theatres and classrooms.

Threshold concept   The idea of a portal that opens up a way of thinking that was previously inaccessible (Meyer and Land, 2003a; 2003b; 2003c).

Transition   Shifts in learner experience caused by a challenge to the person's life world. Transitions occur in particular areas of students' lives, at different times and in distinct ways. The notion of transitions carries with it the idea of movement from one place to another and with it the necessity of taking up a new position in a different place.

Transitional learning   Learning that occurs as a result of critical reflection upon shifts (transitions) that have taken place for the students personally (including viscerally), pedagogically and/or interactionally.

Troublesome knowledge   Perkins (1999) described conceptually difficult knowledge as 'troublesome knowledge'. This is knowledge that appears, for example, counterintuitive, alien (emanating from another culture or discourse) or incoherent (discrete aspects are unproblematic but there is no organizing principle).

Troublesome spaces   places where 'stuckness' or 'disjunction' occurs.

Virtual learning environment (VLE)   A set of learning and teaching tools, involving online technology, designed to enhance students' learning experience, for example Blackboard, WebCT.

Wikis   Server software that allows multiple users to contribute to a website.

Writing spaces   Opportunities not only to write but to reconsider one's stances and ideas. The notion of writing spaces is not acultural or apolitical and is clearly located in understandings of identity and the way in which language, concepts and symbols are integrated by the individual.

References

Alexander, B. (2006) Web 2.0: a new wave of innovation for teaching and learning? *Educause Review*, 41(2). www.educause.edu/apps/er/erm06/erm0621.asp (accessed 26 Oct. 2006).

Ashwin, P. (2005) Variation in students' experiences of the Oxford Tutorial, *Higher Education*, 50: 631–44.

Ausubel, D.P., Novak, J.S. and Hanesian, H. (1978) *Educational Psychology: A Cognitive View*. New York: Holt, Rinehart and Winston.

Bakhtin, M.M. (1981) *The Dialogic Imagination, Four Essays*, trans. C. Emerson and M. Holquist. Austin, TX: University of Texas Press.

Bakhtin, M.M. (1984) *Problems of Dostoevsky's Poetics*. Manchester: Manchester University Press.

Bandyopadhyay, P. (1989) *Rabindranath Tagore*. Calcutta: Anglia.

Barnett, R. (1997) *Higher Education: A Critical Business*. Buckingham: Open University Press/SRHE.

Barnett, R. (2000) *Realizing the University in an Age of Supercomplexity*. Buckingham: Open University Press/SRHE.

Barnett, R. (2003) *Beyond all Reason: Living with Ideology in the University*. Buckingham: Open University Press/SRHE.

Barnett, R. (2004) Learning for an unknown future, *Higher Education Research and Development*, 23(3): 247–60.

Barnett, R. and Coate, K. (2002) *Conceptualizing Curricula: A Schema*. Imaginative Curriculum Knowledge Development Paper, 2 April. www.heacademy.ac.uk/1521.htm (accessed 16 Dec. 2006).

Barrett, H. and Carney, J. (2005) *Conflicting Paradigms and Competing Purposes in Electronic Portfolio Development*. www.electronicportfolios.com/portfolios/LEAJournal-BarrettCarney.pdf (accessed 26 Oct. 2006).

Baudrillard, J. (1994) *Simulacra and Simulation*, first published 1981, trans. S. Glaser. Ann Arbor, MI: University of Michigan Press.

Bauman, Z. (2000) *Liquid Modernity*. Cambridge: Polity Press.

Bayne, S. (2004) Smoothness and striation in digital learning spaces, *E-Learning Journal*, 1(2): 302–16.

Bayne, S. (2005a) Deceit, desire and control: the identities of learners and teachers in cyberspace, in R. Land and S. Bayne (eds) *Education in Cyberspace*. London: Routledge.

Bayne, S. (2005b) Higher education as a visual practice: seeing though the virtual learning environment. Paper presented to annual conference of the Society for Research into Higher Education, University of Edinburgh, 13–15 December 2005.

Beck, U. (1992) *Risk Society.* London: Sage.

Belenky, M.F., Clinchy, B.M., Goldberger, N.R. and Tarule, J.M. (1986) *Women's Ways of Knowing.* New York: Basic Books.

Bernstein, B. (1992) Pedagogic identities and educational reform. Mimeo. Paper given to Santiago conference, April.

Bernstein, B. (1996). *Pedagogy Symbolic Control and Identity.* London: Taylor and Francis.

Biggs, J. (1999) *Teaching for Quality Learning at University.* Buckingham: SRHE/Open University Press.

Bloom, B. (1956) *Taxonomy of Educational Objectives.* 2 vols. New York: Longmans Green.

Bodington Open Source Project, http://bodington.org/index.php (accessed 6 Dec. 2006).

Bolton, G. (1999) *The Therapeutic Potential of Creative Writing. Writing Myself.* London: Jessica Kingsley.

Boud, D., Cohen, R. and Walker, D. (1993) Introduction: understanding learning from experience, in D. Boud, R. Cohen and D. Walker (eds) *Using Experience for Learning.* Buckingham: Open University Press/SRHE.

Boud, D., Keogh, R. and Walker, D. (eds) (1985) *Reflection: Turning Experience into Learning.* London: Kogan Page.

Boughey, C. (2006) Texts, practices and students learning: a view from the South. Keynote speech Higher Education CloseUp3, University of Lancaster, 24–26 July.

Bourdieu, P. (1975) The specificity of the scientific field and the social conditions of progress of reason, *Social Science Information*, 14(6): 299–316.

Bruns, A. (2007) Beyond difference: reconfiguring education for the user-led age. Paper presented at Ideas in Cyberspace Education, 3 Ross Priory, Loch Lomond, 21–23 March. www.education.ed.ac.uk/ice3/papers/bruns.html (accessed 16 Apr. 2007).

Bruns, A. and Humphreys, S. (2005) Wikis in teaching and assessment: the M>cyclopedia project, *Proceedings of WikiSym 2005.* http://snurb.info/files/Wikis%20in%20Teaching%20and%20Assessment.pdf (accessed 26 Oct. 2006).

Buber, M. (1964) *Daniel: Dialogues on Realization.* New York: Holt, Rinehart and Winston.

Burbules, N.C. (1997) Aporia: webs, passages, getting lost, and learning to go on, *Philosophy of Education Year Book.* www.ed.uiuc.edu/eps/pes-yearbook/97_docs/burbules.html (accessed 6 Nov. 2006).

Byrne, D. (2005) Complexity, configuration and cases, *Theory, Culture and Society*, 22(5): 95–111.

Cairns, L. and Stephenson, J. (2002) Online workplace learning: ideas, issues and a 'working example'. Paper delivered at American Educational Research Association conference, April. www.johnstephenson.net/jsdownloads.htm (accessed 5 Dec. 2006).

Carroll, J. (2002) *A Handbook for Deterring Plagiarism in Higher Education.* Oxford: Oxford Centre for Staff and Learning Development.

Castells, M. (1996) *The Information Age: Economy, Society and Culture*, Vol. 1. Oxford: Blackwell.

Clandinin, D.J. and Connelly, F.M. (1994) Personal experience methods, in N.K. Denzin and Y.S. Lincoln (eds) *Handbook of Qualitative Research*. Thousand Oaks, CA: Sage.

Cockburn, C. (1998) *The Space Between Us. Negotiating Gender and National Identities in Conflict*. London: Zed Books.

Cohn, E. and Hibbitts, B. (2004) Beyond the electronic portfolio: a lifetime personal web space, *Educause Quarterly*, 27(4). www.educause.edu/apps/eq/eqm04/eqm0441.asp (accessed 26 Oct. 2006).

Coleridge, S.T ([1817] 1983) *Biographia Literaria*. Princeton, NJ: Princeton University Press.

Cook, J. (2007) Smells like teen spirit: generation CX. Paper presented at Ideas in Cyberspace Education, 3 Ross Priory, Loch Lomond, 21–23 March. www.education.ed.ac.uk/ice3/papers/cook.html (accessed 16 Apr. 2007).

Cooper, A. (2006) I didn't expect a kind of Spanish Inquisition. Paper presented at Staff and Educational Development Conference, Birmingham, November.

Cousin, G. (2005) Learning from cyberspace, in R. Land and S. Bayne (eds) *Education in Cyberspace*. Abingdon: RoutledgeFalmer.

Cousin, G. (2006) Threshold concepts, troublesome knowledge and emotional capital: an exploration into learning about others, in J.H.F. Meyer and R. Land (eds) *Overcoming Barriers to Student Understanding: Threshold Concepts and Troublesome Knowledge*. Abingdon: RoutledgeFalmer.

Crème, P. and Lea, M. (1997) *Writing at University*. Buckingham: Open University Press.

Csikszentmihalyi, M. (1996) *Creativity: Flow and the Psychology of Discovery and Invention*. New York: Harper Perennial.

Davies, P. (2006) Threshold concepts. How can we recognize them? in J.H.F. Meyer and R. Land (eds) *Overcoming Barriers to Student Understanding: Threshold Concepts and Troublesome Knowledge*. Abingdon: RoutledgeFalmer.

Deleuze, G. and Guattari, F. (1987) *On the Line*, trans. J. Johnston. New York: Semiotexte.

Deleuze, G. and Guattari, F. (1988) *A Thousand Plateaus: Capitalism and Schizophrenia*. London: Continuum.

Denzin, N.K. (1989) *Interpretive Biography*. Newbury Park, CA: Sage.

Dill, D. (2005) The degradation of the academic ethic: teaching, research and self regulation. Keynote speech to Society for Research in Higher Education conference, 16–18 December. www.unc.edu/ppaq/docs/SRHE5.pdf (accessed 5 Dec. 2006).

Douglas, M. (2002) Civic spaces in a global age: an agenda for Pacific Asia cities. Paper presented at Forum on Civic Spaces in the Cities of Asia-Pacific, Singapore, 4–5 March. (available at www.bp.ntu.edu.tw/bpwww/Students/course/92_2/hcj/CivicSpace_MD.pdf (accessed 29 Oct. 2006).

Durkheim, E. (1952) *Suicide: A Study in Sociology*, trans. from the French by J.A. Spaulding and G. Simpson. London: Routledge and Kegan Paul.

Edwards, R. (1997) *Changing Places? Flexibility, Lifelong Learning and a Learning Society*. London: Routledge.

Ellsworth, E. (1997) *Teaching Positions: Difference, Pedagogy and the Power of Address*. New York: Teachers College Press.

Entwistle, N. (2006) Threshold concepts within research into higher education. Paper presented to Threshold Concepts in the Disciplines Symposium, University of Strathclyde, 30 August–1 September.

Eriksen, T.H. (2001) *Tyranny of the Moment: Fast and Slow Time in the Information Age.* London: Pluto Press.

Falk, C. (1999) Sentencing learners to life: retrofitting the academy for the information age, *Theory, Technology and Culture,* 22(1–2). www.ctheory.net/articles. aspx?id=113 (accessed 30 Nov. 2006).

Faulks, S. (2005) *Human Traces.* London: Vintage.

Feenberg, A. (1989) The written world: on the theory and practice of computer conferencing, in R. Mason and A. Kaye (eds) *Mindweave: Communication, Computers and Distance Education.* Elmsford, NY: Pergamon Press.

Ferreday, D. and Hodgson, V. (2007) Role of emotion in online learning and knowledge production. Paper presented at Ideas in Cyberspace Education, 3 Ross Priory, Loch Lomond, 21–23 March. www.education.ed.ac.uk/ice3/papers/ ferredayhodgson.html (accessed 16 Apr. 2007).

Flecha, R. (2000) *Sharing Words: Theory and Practice of Dialogic Learning.* Lanham, MD: Rowman and Littlefield.

Freire, P. (1974) *Education: The Practice of Freedom.* London: Writers and Readers Co-operative.

Fuller, S. (2006) Disciplinary boundaries and intellectual autonomy – an essential tension. Keynote speech at Society for Research into Higher Education, Brighton, 13 December. www2.warwick.ac.uk/fac/soc/sociology/staff/academic/fullers/ fullers_index/audio (accessed 15 Dec. 2006).

Gadotti, M. (1996) *Pedagogy of Praxis: A Dialectical Philosophy of Education.* Albany, NY: State University of New York Press.

Game, A. and Metcalf, A. (1996) *Passionate Sociology.* London: Sage.

Gee, J.P. (2004) *What Video Games Have to Teach Us about Learning and Literacy.* Basingstoke: Palgrave Macmillan.

Gee, J.P. (n.d) *The New Literacy Studies and the 'Social Turn'.* www.schools.ash.org.au/ litweb/page300.html (accessed 6 Dec. 2006).

Gibbons, M., Limoges, C., Nowotny, H., Schwarzman, S., Scott, P. and Trow, M. (1994) *The New Production of Knowledge: The Dynamics of Science and Research in Contemporary Societies.* London: Sage.

Gibran, K. (1994) *The Prophet.* London: Senate Books.

Giddens, A. (1991) *The Consequences of Modernity.* Stanford, CA: Stanford University Press.

Giroux, H.A and Giroux, S. (2004) *Take Back Higher Education.* London: Palgrave.

Goleman, D. (1995) *Emotional Intelligence.* New York: Bantam Books.

Gutiérrez, K., Baquedano-Lopez, P. and Tejeda, C. (1999). Rethinking diversity: hybridity and hybrid language practices in the third space, *Mind, Culture, and Activity: An International Journal,* 6(4): 286–303.

Habermas, J. (1972) *Knowledge and Human Interests.* London: Heinemann.

Habermas, J. (1984) *The Theory of Communicative Action,* Vol. 1. Cambridge: Polity Press.

Habermas, J. (1987) *The Theory of Communicative Action,* Vol. 2. Cambridge: Polity Press.

Haggis, T. (2004) Meaning, identity and 'motivation': expanding what matters in understanding learning in higher education? *Studies in Higher Education,* 29(3): 335–52.

Haggis, T. (2006) Problems and paradoxes in 'fine-grained qualitative research': an exploration of 'context' from the perspective of complexity and dynamic systems theory, paper presented at *Higher Education Close Up* conference, Lancaster, July.

Hall, S. (1996). Introduction: who needs 'identity'? in S. Hall and P. du Gay (eds) *Questions of Cultural Identity.* London: Sage.

Haraway, D. (1991) *Simians, Cyborgs, and Women: The Reinvention of Nature.* London: Routledge.

Harris Interactive (2006) *Email, Research, News and Weather, Information about Hobbies or Special Interests Top the List of How People Use the Internet as it Continues to Grow.* www.harrisinteractive.com/harris_poll/index.asp?PID=527 (accessed 15 Dec. 2006).

Herring, S. (2004) Slouching toward the ordinary: current trends in computer-mediated communication, *New Media and Society,* 6(1): 26–36.

Howard, R. (2001) Plagiarism: what should a teacher do? Paper presented at the Conference on College Composition and Communication, Denver, Colorado, 17 March. http://wrt-howard.syr.edu/Papers/CCCC2001.html (accessed 6 Dec. 2006).

Husserl, E. (1937/1970). *The Crisis of the European Sciences and Transcendental Phenomenology,* trans. D. Carr. Evanston, IL: Northwestern University Press.

Jameson, F. (1991) *Postmodernism or the Cultural Logic of Late Capitalism.* London: Verso.

Jenkins, A. and Zetter, R. (2003) *Linking Teaching and Research in Departments.* York: Higher Education Academy. www.heacademy.ac.uk/resources.asp?process=full_record&section=generic&id=257 (accessed 16 Dec. 2006).

Jewitt, C. (2005) Multimodality, 'reading' and 'writing' for the 21st century. *Discourse: Studies in the Cultural Politics of Education,* 26(3): 315–31.

Jones, C.R. (2005) Nobody knows you're a dog, in R. Land and S. Bayne (eds) *Education in Cyberspace.* London: RoutledgeFalmer.

Joyce, J. (1922) *Ulysses.* London: Penguin Modern Classics (paperback, 2000).

Jung, K. (1977) *The Symbolic Life: Miscellaneous Writings The Collected Works of C. G. Jung,* Vol. 18. Princeton, NJ: Princeton University Press.

Kandlbinder, P. and Mauffette, Y. (2001) Perceptions of teaching by science teachers using a students-centred approach. The power of problem-based learning. Refereed proceedings of the 3rd Asia Pacific Conference on Problem-based Learning, Rockhampton, 9–12 December.

Kubler-Ross, E. (1973) *On Death and Dying.* London: Routledge.

Land, R. (2004) *Educational Development, Discourse, Identity and Practice.* Maidenhead: SRHE/Open University Press.

Land, R. (2006) Paradigms lost: academic practice and exteriorising technologies, *E-Learning,* 3(1): 100–10.

Land, R. and Bayne, S. (2005) Screen or monitor? Issues of surveillance and disciplinary power in online learning environments, in R. Land and S. Bayne (eds) *Education in Cyberspace.* London: RoutledgeFalmer.

Land, R. and Bayne, S. (2006) Issues in cyberspace education, in M. Savin-Baden and K. Wilkie (eds) *Problem-based Learning Online.* Maidenhead: McGraw-Hill.

Land, R., Cousin, G., Meyer, J.H.F. and Davies, P. (2005) Threshold concepts and troublesome knowledge (3): implications for course design and evaluation, in C. Rust (ed.), *Improving Student Learning 12 – Diversity and Inclusivity.* Oxford: Oxford Brookes University.

Landow, G. (1997) *Hypertext 2.0: The Convergence of Contemporary Critical Theory and Technology.* London: Johns Hopkins University Press.

Lee, S. (n.d.) *Finally, a Free Lunch: The Benefits of an Open Source VLE.* http://bodington.org/art_opensource_vle.pdf (accessed 29 Oct. 2006).

Lefebvre, H. (1991) *The Production of Space*, 15th edn. Oxford: Blackwell.

Light, G. and Cox, R. (2001) *Learning and Teaching in Higher Education*. London: Paul Chapman Publishing.

Lorenzo, T., Duncan, M., Buchanan, H. and Alsop, A. (eds) (2006) *Practice and Service Learning in Occupational Therapy: Enhancing Potential in Context*. Chichester: John Wiley and Sons.

Lorris, G. de (1270–7) 'Roman de la Rose'. www.gutenberg.org/etext/16816 (accessed 12 Dec. 2006).

Lyotard, J.-F. (1979) *The Postmodern Condition: A Report on Knowledge*. www.marxists.org/reference/subject/philosophy/works/fr/lyotard.htm (accessed 17 Jul. 2007).

Macfarlane, B. (2005) The disengaged academic – the retreat from citizenship, *Higher Education Quarterly*, 59(4): 296–312.

Malcolm, J. and Zukas, M. (2005) The imaginary workplace: academics as workplace learners. Proceedings of the 4th International Conference on Researching Work and Learning, University of Technology Sydney. www.oval.uts.edu.au/rwl4/ (accessed 12 Dec. 2006).

Manathunga, C. (2006) Doing educational development ambivalently: applying postcolonial metaphors to educational development, *International Journal for Academic Development*, 11(1): 19–29.

Mandela, N. (1994) *The Long Walk to Freedom*. London: Abacus.

Marton, F. and Säljö, R. (1984) Approaches to learning, in F. Marton, D. Hounsell and N.J. Entwistle (eds) *The Experience of Learning*. Edinburgh: Scottish Academic Press.

McAlpine, M. (2005) E-portfolios and digital identity: some issues for discussion, *E-Learning*, 2(4): 378–87.

McCarron, K. (2006) Its no joke! Stand-up comedy and the seminar. Paper presented at Society for Research into Higher Education, Brighton, 13 December.

McCarron, K. and Savin-Baden, M, (2007) Compering and comparing: stand-up comedy and pedagogy, *Innovations in Education and Teaching International*, forthcoming.

McNay, I. (1995) From the collegial academy to corporate enterprise: the changing cultures of universities, in T. Schuller (ed.) *The Changing University?* Buckingham: Open University Press/SRHE.

McWilliam, E. (2004) Changing the academic subject, *Studies in Higher Education*, 29(2): 151–63.

McWilliam, E. (2005) Unlearning pedagogy. Keynote speech presented to ICE2 Ideas in Cyberspace Education, Higham Hall, Keswick, 23–25 February.

Meyer, J.H.F. and Eley, M.G. (2006) The approaches to teaching inventory: a critique of its development and applicability, *British Journal of Education Psychology*, 76: 633–49.

Meyer, J.H.F. and Land, R. (2003a) Threshold concepts and troublesome knowledge (1): linkages to ways of thinking and practising within the disciplines, in C. Rust (ed.) *Improving Student Learning: Theory and Practice – Ten Years On*. Oxford: Oxford Centre for Staff and Learning Development.

Meyer, J.H.F. and Land, R. (2003b) Threshold concepts and troublesome knowledge: linkages to ways of thinking and practising within the disciplines, in C. Rust (ed.) *Improving Student Learning: Theory and Practice – 10 Years On*. Proceedings of the 10th Improving Student Learning Conference. pp. 412–424. Oxford: OCLSD.

Meyer, J.H.F. and Land, R. (2003c) *Threshold Concepts and Troublesome Knowledge:*

Linkages to Ways of Thinking and Practising within the Disciplines, ETL Project Occasional Report, No. 4. www.ed.ac.uk/etl/publications.html (accessed 10 Jul. 2007).

Meyer, J.H.F. and Land, R. (2005) Threshold concepts and troublesome knowledge (2): Epistemological considerations and a conceptual framework for teaching and learning, *Higher Education*, 49(3): 373–88.

Meyer, J.H.F. and Land, R. (2006) Threshold concepts and troublesome knowledge: issues of liminality, in J.H.F. Meyer and R. Land (eds) *Overcoming Barriers to Student Understanding: Threshold Concepts and Troublesome Knowledge*. Abingdon: RoutledgeFalmer.

Mezirow, J. (1981) A critical theory of adult learning and education, *Adult Education*, 32: 3–24.

Mezirow, J. (1985) 'A critical theory of self-directed learning', in S. Brookfield (ed.) *Self-Directed Learning: From Theory to Practice*. San Francisco, CA: Jossey-Bass.

Mezirow, J. (1991) *Transformative Dimensions of Adult Learning*. San Francisco, CA: Jossey-Bass.

Midgley, M. (1994) *The Ethical Primate*. London: Routledge.

Mills, D. (2006) Science = vocation[2]? Rethinking the academic 'career' in the social sciences. Paper presented to Higher Education Close Up 3, University of Lancaster, 24–26 July. www.lancs.ac.uk/fss/events/hecu3/papershecu3.htm (accessed 12 Oct. 2006).

Moore, R. and Young, M. (2001) Knowledge and the curriculum in the sociology of education: towards a reconceptualisation. *British Journal of Sociology of Education*, 22(4): 445–61.

Murray, R. (2005) *Writing for Academic Journals*. Maidenhead: McGraw-Hill.

Nelson, L. (1949) *Socratic Method and Critical Philosophy: Selected Essays*. New York: Dover Press.

Nespor, J. (2006) Classrooms and extended networks of schooling – comments for plenary session, Ethnography and Education Research Forum, University of Pennyslvania, Philadelphia, 25 February.

Nixon, J. (2005) Education for the good society: the integrity of academic practice. Paper published November 2004 in *London Review of Education* (Special Issue: Renewing Education for Civic Society) 2(3): 245–52, presented at the ESRC/ TLRP Seminar on 'conceptions of professionalism and professional knowledge', King College London, 16 May.

O'Neill, O. (2002) *A Question of Trust* (The BBC Reith Lectures). Cambridge: Cambridge University Press.

O'Reilly, D. (1989) On being an educational fantasy engineer: incoherence, the individual and independent study, in S. Weil and I. McGill (eds) *Making Sense of Experiential Learning: Diversity in Theory and Practice*. Buckingham: Open University Press/SRHE.

O'Reilly, T. (2005) What is Web 2.0? Design patterns and business models for the next generation of software. www.oreillynet.com/pub/a/oreilly/tim/news/2005/ 09/30/what-is-web-20.html?page=1 (accessed 29 Oct. 2006).

Papert, S. (1986) *Constructionism: A New Opportunity for Elementary Science Education. Proposal to the National Science Foundations*. Cambridge, MA: MIT Media Laboratory.

Pask, G. (1976) Styles and strategies of learning, *British Journal of Educational Psychology*, 46: 128–48.

Pecorari, D. (2003) Good and original: plagiarism and patchwriting in academic second-language writing, *Journal of Second Language Writing*, 12: 317–45.

Pelletier, C. (2005) New technologies, new identities: the university in the informational age, in R. Land and S. Bayne (eds) *Education in Cyberspace*. London: RoutledgeFalmer.

Perkins, D. (1999) The many faces of constructivism, *Educational Leadership*, 57(3): 6–11.

Perkins, D. (2006a) Beyond understanding. Keynote paper presented to Threshold Concepts in the Disciplines Symposium, University of Strathclyde, 30 August.

Perkins, D. (2006b) Constructivism and troublesome knowledge, in J.H.F. Meyer and R. Land (eds) *Overcoming Barriers to Student Understanding: Threshold Concepts and Troublesome Knowledge*. Abingdon: RoutledgeFalmer.

Perry, W.G. (1970) *Forms of Intellectual and Ethical Development During the College Years: A Scheme*. New York: Holt, Rinehart and Winston.

Perry, W.G. (1981) Cognitive and ethical growth: the making of meaning, in A.W. Chickering (ed.) *The Modern American College: Responding to the New Realities of Diverse Students and a Changing Society*. San Francisco, CA: Jossey-Bass.

Philips, E. and Pugh, D. (1987) *How to Get a PhD*. Buckingham: SRHE/Open University Press.

Phipps, A. (2005) The sound of higher education. Accompanying text of the closing keynote lecture given at the annual conference of the Society for Research into Higher Education, University of Edinburgh, 15 December.

Piaget, J. (1928) *Judgement and Reasoning in the Child*. New York: Harcourt Brace.

Piaget, J. (1929) *The Child's Conception of the World*. London: Routledge and Kegan Paul.

Potter, J. and Wetherell, M. (1987) *Discourse and Social Psychology*. London: Sage.

Prensky, M. (2001) Digital natives, digital immigrants, *On the Horizon*, 9(5): 1–6.

Ramsden. P. (1984) The context of learning, in F. Marton, D. Hounsell and N.J. Entwistle (eds) *The Experience of Learning*. Edinburgh: Scottish Academic Press.

Ramsden, P. (1992) *Learning to Teach in Higher Education*. London: Routledge.

Readings, B. (1997) *The University in Ruins*. Cambridge, MA: Harvard University Press.

Reid, I. (1996) *Higher Education or Education for Hire? Language and Values in Australian Universities*. Rockhampton, Queensland: Central Queensland University Press.

Rieber, L.P., Smith, L. and Noah, D. (1998) The value of serious play, *Educational Technology*, 38(6): 29–37.

Rogers, C. (1983) *Freedom to Learn for the '80's*. Columbus, OH: Merrill.

Rosenberg, M.E. (1994) Physics and hypertext: liberation and complicity in art and pedagogy, in G. Landow (ed.) *Hyper/text/theory*. Baltimore, MD: Johns Hopkins University Press.

Ross, K. (2005) Woman in the byzone, in S. Allan (ed.) *Journalism: Critical Issues*. Maidenhead: McGraw-Hill.

Ross, K. and Carter, C. (2004) A woman's place? Gender and culture in higher education, *Knowledge, Work and Society*, 2(3): 97–115.

Russell, W. (1983) *Educating Rita*. Columbia Pictures.

Ryle, G. (1949) *The Concept of Mind*. Harmondsworth: Penguin (reprinted 1968).

Saljo, R. (1979) *Learning in the Learner's Perspective. 1. Some Common-sense Conceptions (Report 76)*. Gothenburg: University of Gothenburg, Department of Education.

Salovey, P. and Mayer, J.D. (1990) Emotional intelligence, *Imagination, Cognition and Personality*, 9: 165–211.

Savin-Baden, M. (2000) *Problem-based Learning in Higher Education: Untold Stories*. Buckingham: SRHE/Open University Press.

Savin-Baden, M. (2003) *Facilitating Problem-Based Learning: Illuminating Perspectives*. Maidenhead: SRHE and Open University Press.

Schmidt, H.G. and Moust, J. (2000) Towards a taxonomy of problems used in problem-based learning curricula, *Journal on Excellence in College Teaching*, 11(2/3): 57–72.

Schön, D.A. (1983) *How Professionals Think in Action*. New York: Basic Books.

Schumpeter, J. (1934) *The Theory of Economic Development*. Cambridge, MA: Harvard University Press.

Seymour, W. (2001) In the flesh or online? Exploring qualitative research methodologies, *Qualitative Research*, 1: 147–68.

Shakespeare, W. (1601) *Hamlet, Prince of Denmark*. www.19.5degs.com/ebook/hamlet-prince-of-denmark/627/read#list (accessed 1 Dec. 2006).

Sharples, M., Taylor, J. and Vavoula, G. (2005) Towards a theory of mobile learning. Paper presented at mLearn 2005, Capetown. www.mlearn.org.za/CD/papers/Sharples-%20Theory%20of%20Mobile.pdf (accessed 31 Oct. 2006).

Shulman, L. (1986) Those who understand: knowledge growth in teaching, *Educational Researcher*, 15(2): 4–14.

Shulman, L. (1987) Knowledge and teaching: foundations of the new reform, *Harvard Educational Review*, 57(1): 1–22.

Shulman, L. (2005a) The signature pedagogies of the professions of law, medicine, engineering, and the clergy: potential lessons for the education of teachers. Paper presented at the Teacher Education for Effective Teaching and Learning workshop hosted by the National Research Council's Center for Education, 8 February. http://hub.mspnet.org/index.cfm/11172 (accessed 16 Dec. 2006).

Shulman, L.S. (2005b) Signature pedagogies in the professions, *Daedalus*, 134(3): 52–9.

Sibbett, C. (2006) Nettlesome knowledge, liminality and the taboo in cancer and art therapy experiences. Paper presented to Threshold Concepts in the Disciplines Symposium, University of Strathclyde, 30 August–1 September.

Sinclair, C. (2006) *Understanding University: A Guide to Another Planet*. Maidenhead: McGraw-Hill.

Smyth, J., Hattam, R., McInerney, P. and Lawson, M. (1997) Finding the 'enunciative space' for teacher leadership and teacher learning in schools. Paper presented at the Australian Association for Research in Education Conference, Brisbane. www.aare.edu.au/97pap/smytj118.htm (accessed 1 Dec. 2006).

Soja, E. (1989) *Postmodern Geographies: The Assertion of Space in Critical Social Theory*. London: Verso.

Soler, M. and Racionero, S. (2004) Dialogic reading: learning to read with the community. Paper presented at the American Educational Research Association Enhancing the Visibility and Credibility of Educational Research, San Diego, 12–16 April. http://convention.allacademic.com/aera2004/view_paper_infoh-html?pub_id=7431andpart_id1=908832 (accessed 11 Oct. 2006).

Spivak, G. (1988) Can the subaltern speak? in C. Nelson and L. Grossberg (eds) *Marxism and the Interpretation of Culture*. Urbana, IL: University of Illinois Press.

Stenhouse, L. (1975) *An Introduction to Curriculum Research and Development*. London: Heinemann.

Stephenson, J. (2002) *The Capability Envelope: A Framework for a Negotiated Curriculum*. Imaginative Curriculum Knowledge Development Paper, 2 April. www.heacademy.ac.uk/1521.htm (accessed 15 Dec. 2006).

Streeter, T., Hintlian, N., Chipetz, S. and Callender, S. (2002) *This Is Not Sex: A Web Essay on the Male Gaze, Fashion Advertising, and the Pose.* www.uvm.edu/%7Etstreete/powerpose/ (accessed 20 Nov. 2006).

Swan, E. (forthcoming) You make me feel like a woman: therapeutic cultures and the contagion of femininity, *Gender, Work and Organisation.*

Tambiah, S.J. (1985) *Culture, Thought and Social Action: An Anthropological Perspective.* Cambridge, MA: Harvard University Press.

Taylor, P.G. (1999) *Making Sense of Academic Life: Academics, Universities and Change.* Buckingham: SRHE and Open University Press.

Taylor, R., Barr, J. and Steele, T. (2002) *For a Radical Higher Education: After Postmodernism.* Buckingham: SRHE and Open University Press.

Temple, P., Barnett, R., Coate, K. and Becker, R. (2007) *Learning spaces for the 21st century.* www.heacademy.ac.uk/4863.htm (accessed 16 Sep. 2007).

Thomas, S. (2005) *Voices from Everywhere.* web.mit.edu/comm-forum/mit4/papers/thomas.pdf (accessed 29 Oct. 2006).

Tolman, E.C. (1948) Cognitive maps in rats and men, *Psychological Review,* 55: 189–208.

Tosh, D., Light, T.P., Fleming, K. and Haywood, J. (2005) Engagement with electronic portfolios: challenges from the student perspective, *Canadian Journal of Learning and Technology,* 31(3). www.cjlt.ca/content/vol31.3/tosh.html (accessed 20 Oct. 2006).

Trigwell, K. and Ashwin P. (2006) An exploratory study of situated conceptions of learning and learning environments, *Higher Education,* 51(2): 243–58.

Trigwell, K., Prosser, M. and Waterhouse, F. (1999) Relations between teachers' approaches to teaching and students' approaches to learning, *Higher Education,* 37: 57–70.

Trow, M. (1974) Problems in the transition from elite to mass higher education, in *Policies for Higher Education, Conference on Future Structures of Postsecondary Education.* Paris: Organisation for Economic Co-operation and Development.

Trubshaw, B. (2003) *The Metaphors and Rituals of Place and Time – An Introduction to Liminality or Why Christopher Robin Wouldn't Walk on the Cracks.* (First published in *Mercian Mysteries,* No. 22, February 1995.) www.indigogroup.co.uk/edge/liminal.htm (accessed 15 Dec. 2006).

Turner, V. (1969) *The Ritual Process: Structure and Anti-Structure.* London: Routledge.

Ulmer, G. (2003) *Web Supplement to Internet Invention.* www.nwe.ufl.edu/~gulmer/longman/pedagogy/electracy.html (accessed 1 May 2006).

Vygotsky, L.S. (1978) *Mind in Society: The Development of Higher Psychological Processes.* Cambridge, MA: Harvard University Press (first published 1930).

Winter, R., Buck, A. and Sobiechowska, P. (1999) *Professional Experience and the Investigative Imagination.* London: Routledge.

Woolf, V. (1931) Professions for women, in V. Woolf, *Women and Writing.* London: Women's Press.

Woolf, V. (1940) *Roger Fry: A Biography.* Orlando, FL: Harcourt Brace Jovanovich.

Index

The Society for Research into Higher Education

The Society for Research into Higher Education (SRHE), an international body, exists to stimulate and co-ordinate research into all aspects of higher education. It aims to improve the quality of higher education through the encouragement of debate and publication on issues of policy, on the organization and management of higher education institutions, and on the curriculum, teaching and learning methods.

The Society is entirely independent and receives no subsidies, although individual events often receive sponsorship from business or industry. The Society is financed through corporate and individual subscriptions and has members from many parts of the world. It is an NGO of UNESCO.

Under the imprint *SRHE & Open University Press*, the Society is a specialist publisher of research, having over 80 titles in print. In addition to *SRHE News*, the Society's newsletter, the Society publishes three journals: *Studies in Higher Education* (three issues a year), *Higher Education Quarterly* and *Research into Higher Education Abstracts* (three issues a year).

The Society runs frequent conferences, consultations, seminars and other events. The annual conference in December is organized at and with a higher education institution. There are a growing number of networks which focus on particular areas of interest, including:

Access	FE/HE
Assessment	Graduate Employment
Consultants	New Technology for Learning
Curriculum Development	Postgraduate Issues
Eastern European	Quantitative Studies
Educational Development Research	Student Development

Benefits to members

Individual

- The opportunity to participate in the Society's networks
- Reduced rates for the annual conferences
- Free copies of *Research into Higher Education Abstracts*
- Reduced rates for *Studies in Higher Education*

- Reduced rates for *Higher Education Quarterly*
- Free online access to *Register of Members' Research Interests* – includes valuable reference material on research being pursued by the Society's members
- Free copy of occasional in-house publications, e.g. *The Thirtieth Anniversary Seminars Presented by the Vice-Presidents*
- Free copies of *SRHE News* and *International News* which inform members of the Society's activities and provides a calendar of events, with additional material provided in regular mailings
- A 35 per cent discount on all SRHE/Open University Press books
- The opportunity for you to apply for the annual research grants
- Inclusion of your research in the *Register of Members' Research Interests*

Corporate

- Reduced rates for the annual conference
- The opportunity for members of the Institution to attend SRHE's network events at reduced rates
- Free copies of *Research into Higher Education Abstracts*
- Free copies of *Studies in Higher Education*
- Free online access to *Register of Members' Research Interests* – includes valuable reference material on research being pursued by the Society's members
- Free copy of occasional in-house publications
- Free copies of *SRHE News* and *International News*
- A 35 per cent discount on all SRHE/Open University Press books
- The opportunity for members of the Institution to submit applications for the Society's research grants
- The opportunity to work with the Society and co-host conferences
- The opportunity to include in the *Register of Members' Research Interests* your Institution's research into aspects of higher education

Membership details: SRHE, 76 Portland Place, London W1B 1NT, UK Tel: 020 7637 2766. Fax: 020 7637 2781. email: srheoffice@srhe.ac.uk
world wide web: http://www.srhe.ac.uk./srhe/
Catalogue: SRHE & Open University Press, McGraw-Hill Education, McGraw-Hill House, Shoppenhangers Road, Maidenhead, Berkshire SL6 2QL. Tel: 01628 502500. Fax: 01628 770224. email: enquiries@openup.co.uk – web: www.openup.co.uk

A WILL TO LEARN
BEING A STUDENT IN AN AGE OF UNCERTAINTY

Ronald Barnett

There is an extraordinary but largely unnoticed phenomenon in higher education: by and large, students persevere and complete their studies. How should we interpret this tendency? Students are living in uncertain times and often experience anxiety, and yet they continue to press forward with their studies. The argument here is that we should understand this propensity on the part of students to persist through *a will to learn*.

This book examines the structure of what it is to have a will to learn. Here, a language of being, becoming, authenticity, dispositions, voice, air, spirit, inspiration and care is drawn on. As such, this book offers an idea of student development that challenges the dominant views of our age, of curricula understood largely in terms of skill or even of knowledge, and pedagogy understood as bringing off pre-specified 'outcomes'.

The will to learn, though, can be fragile. This is of crucial importance, for if the will to learn dissolves, the student's commitment may falter. Accordingly, more than encouraging an interest in the student's subject or in the acquiring of skills, the *primary* responsibility of teachers in higher education is to sustain and develop the student's will to learn. This is a radical thesis, for it implies a transformation in how we understand the nature of teaching in higher education.

Contents

2007   220pp
978–0–335–22380–0 (Paperback)
978–0–335–22381–7 (Hardback)

PROBLEM-BASED LEARNING ONLINE

Edited by Maggi Savin-Baden and Kay Wilkie

This book makes a great shot at disentangling the challenge of the diversity of learning technologies and their intricate association with pedagogical approaches. The terms used by the book – combining, uniting and inter-relationships – in some ways underplay the major challenges it poses. Have a good read of it – and most importantly try out some ideas.

> Gilly Salmon, Professor of E-learning & Learning Technologies,
> Beyond Distance Research Alliance

This [book] represents a significant collection of papers which, I am sure, will help inform the development of an online pedagogy for problem-based learning.

> Michael Prosser, Director Research and Evaluation,
> Higher Education Academy

The studies presented in this book are evidence informed and theoretically framed in ways that promise to advance our understanding of these complex areas. This collection will be an invaluable read for anyone involved in PBL and/or e-learning in higher education.

> Glynis Cousin, Senior Adviser, Higher Education Academy

Problem-based Learning Online is the first book to:

- Address the current issues and debates about problem-based learning (PBL) online together in one volume
- Present and explore the range and diversity of application of PBL online
- Examine questions such as how course design and issues of power influence learning in PBL

The book provides research-based information about the realities of setting up and running problem-based programmes using technology in a variety of ways. It also captures the diversity of use of technology with PBL across disciplines and countries, providing vital input into the literature on the theory and practice of PBL online.

Contributors

Chris Beaumont, Siân Bayne, Chew Swee Cheng, Frances Deepwell, Sharon J. Derry, Roisin Donnelly, Carolyn Gibbon, Cindy E. Hmelo-Silver, Per Grøttum, David Jennings, Ray Land, Karen Lee, Kirsten Hofgaard Lycke, Anandi Nagarajan, Remy Rikers, Frans Ronteltap, Maggi Savin-Baden, Henk Schmidt, Helge I. Strømsø, Andy Syson, Kay Wilkie, Wilco te Winkel.

Contents

Part 1: Possibilities and challenges – Part 2: Facilitation and mediation – Part 3: Technopedagogy – Part 4: Developing technology – Index.

2006   268pp
978–0–335–22006–9 (Paperback)
978–0–335–22007–6 (Hardback)

CHALLENGING E-LEARNING IN THE UNIVERSITY
A LITERACIES PERSPECTIVE

Robin Goodfellow and Mary R. Lea

Informed by an intimate knowledge of a social literacies perspective, this book is full of profound insights and unexpected connections. Its scholarly, clear-eyed analysis of the role of new media in higher education sets the agenda for e-learning research in the twenty-first century.

Ilana Snyder, Monash University

This book offers a radical rethinking of e-learning . . . The authors challenge teachers, course developers, and policy makers to see e-learning environments as textual practices, rooted deeply in the social and intellectual life of academic disciplines. This approach holds great promise for moving e-learning past its focus on technology and 'the learner' toward vital engagement with fields of inquiry through texts.

Professor David Russell, Iowa State University

Challenging E-learning in the University takes a new approach to the growing field of e-learning in higher education. In it, the authors argue that in order to develop e-learning in the university we need to understand the texts and practices that are involved in learning and teaching using online and web-based technologies.

The book develops an approach which draws together social and cultural approaches to literacies, learning and technologies, illustrating these in practice through the exploration of case studies.

It is key reading for educational developers who are concerned with the promises offered, but rarely delivered, with each new iteration of learning with technologies. It will also be of interest to literacies researchers and to HE policy makers and managers who wish to understand the contexts of e-learning.

Contents
Acknowledgements – Introduction – Approaches to learning: Developing e-learning agendas – Learning technologies in the university: From 'tools for learning' to 'sites of practice' – The social literacies of learning with technologies – The 'university', 'academic' and 'digital' literacies in e-learning – A literacies approach in practice – The literacies of e-learning: Research directions – References – Index.

2007   176pp
978–0–335–22087–8 (Paperback)
978–0–335–22088–5 (Hardback)